Rosemary's Journey

D1506634

My Story: Living life by my standards and on my own terms.

By: C. Rosemary King Major

Illustrations by: Nicolas Valdez

TABLE OF CONTENTS

This book is dedicated to my children whom I love and cherish.

Rose's Journey

(A young mother who didn't hesitate to do what was needed to keep her family together.)

Although she struggled in a city (Chi-Town) that can test your will. She found a way to raise 6 kids and let them know she was the baddest MUTHA in the projects. We all enjoyed our extended family (Papa Dan, Aunt Carrie, Aunt Kate) while growing up. How many times did you lay awake at night trying to put it all together? How many times did you have to decide whether to beat us for doing wrong or share your knowledge to teach us something to make us a better person? Robbins was great place to help us grow and learn that the world is waiting for us to explore it. While some of us have seen more of it than others, we all knew Robbins was not the last stop. Grandmeir is a hat you wear well. All of your grandchildren and great grandchildren LOVE YOU A LOT! Everyone of us have taken many of Rose's life lesson's with us. And I'm sure those lessons will be or have been passed on to our children. The journey has been long and at times very hard. Many times I'm sure you didn't know how you would make it, but you did make it. .

ROSE AS YOUR JOURNEY CONTINUES KNOW THAT
"WE LOVE YOU!"

INTRODUCTION

Rosemary's Journey is not my first published work. It is my second. The first was a poem published in "Highlights," my school's newsletter in April of 1950, when I was eight years old.

This book offers you a glimpse into my life. For the most part, when I look back over my life, I believe that I had more good days than bad, so I am not complaining.

I thank God because He has put some outstanding people in my life. I believe the secret to a happy life is surrounding yourself with good people and I've had so many good people in my life. For this I am truly grateful.

This little memoir may not be much, but it will tell you something about my life, the people I love, and those that made it possible for us to be here today.

Love, Mama, Grandmeir, Rosemary

ONE

MY PARENTS

Above: Virdell & Daniel King, Sr. 1956.

I am the third child born to Virdell and Daniel King. When I arrived, my mother was 23 and my father was 24 years old. My mother, an only child, grew up in Marked Tree, Arkansas and lived with her aunt and uncle, Virginia (Ida) and Charlie Nunn. Mama and Daddy were married in 1936. They attended elementary education together as children.

Prior to 1890, there was a large tree on the bank of the St. Francis River that had been marked (blazed) by Native Americans to identify a shortcut across the land to the "Little River", which branched off of the St. Francis River. The walking distance from this marked tree to the St. Francis River was approximately 120 yards. This shortcut through the woods eliminated the need for the Native American people to paddle 12 miles upstream on the St. Francis River to intersect with the "Little River". The city of Marked Tree got its name because of this marked tree by the riverbank. Marked Tree, Arkansas has frequently been noted on the list of "Unusual Place Names."

In Marked Tree, Arkansas, as well as most cities in the South, they had a dual system for education. This system consisted of one set of schools for White children and a different set of schools for Black children. The first school for Blacks in Marked Tree was George Washington Carver and it was built in 1938 and served the Black community until it was closed in 1966. My mother attended one of the schools designated for the Black students in the early 1930s and received a great education.

As an only child, my mother, Virdell, was accustomed to having everything she wanted. My mother's extended family (aunts and uncles) spoiled her rotten. My maternal grandmother Cornelius Jackson Binston (aka Little Mama) was absent most of my mother's childhood. In addition, my mother never had much communication with her father, Willie Binston (aka Kid Lightening). However, she did know him.

Virdell and Daniel King began having children shortly after marrying. My oldest sister is Bettie and was named after our great grandmother (Bettie Jackson) and our paternal grandmother (Gillie King). Her full name at birth was Bettie Gillie Virginia King. Bettie was also named after my mother's aunt Virginia that raised her. My brother goes by the name of Jimmy, but his full name is Daniel Leon King Junior.

When I was born my mother named me Cornelius after her mother. My middle name (Rosemary) is the combined names of Rose and Mary. Rose came from Rosetta who was Little Mama's sister. The name Mary is after Aunt Mary,

Little Mama's other sister . . . Hence: Rosemary. Many in my family call me "May". It was very important to my parents to honor their relatives by naming their children after them. By the time my sister Cassie Marie was born, they were out of female relatives to name her after. So, Cassie was named after the woman that my mother worked for.

Most people are born with a birthmark. I was born with a skin tag on my left ear. Over the years, many have asked me about the skin tag on my left ear. According to my mother, her father was shot in the head right in the spot where I have my skin tag. My mother states that when she went to see his body at the funeral home, she took her finger and covered the scar where he had been shot. Mama was pregnant with me when she visited her father's body at the funeral home. She swore until her dying day that this is why I have a skin tag in that very place. I believed this explanation until my grandson Ryan was born. Ryan is my daughter L'Tonya's son and he too was born with a skin tag on his ear. So now I'm not so sure where my skin tag originated.

According to family rumors, Mama often told people she had three children, but one was "burnt". What she meant by that was that her other children were of lighter complexion. My skin pigment is darker than my mother, sister and brother's complexion. While I resemble both of my parents, my complexion is the same as my father's complexion. For many people of color, one's complexion is something that has often been an issue and at the forefront of conversations

Virdell and Daniel had a rocky marriage. When Mama got mad, she would go back to her aunt and uncle's home. On one of those occasions, when I was one-and-a-half or two years old, Mama took my sister, brother, and me to Maw-Maw and Paw-Paw's house in Memphis, Tennessee. Maw-Maw and Paw-Paw (Gillie and Walter King) were my father's parents and they had moved from Marked Tree to Memphis.

Mama sat me on the front porch, along with my sister and brother, and told Maw-Maw and Paw-Paw, "Since Dan feels I am not good enough to raise his children, then he can raise them himself." Some time passed and Mama came back to Memphis to get my older sister and brother because she had another baby and she needed my sister to help take care of the baby. I stayed with Maw-Maw and Paw-Paw until I was about four years old. When Mama left this time, she took my brother and sister to her new home in Hot Springs, Arkansas. I can remember visiting my mother in Hot Springs and also going to a wedding there. What I remember most was that I wanted to live with my mother, brother and sister. Decades later after my mother passed, my sister found a letter written by Maw-Maw to Aunt Virginia, my grandmother's sister that raised my mother. In the letter, Maw-Maw told Aunt Virginia that I was asking to go live with my brother and sister.

On the day that I left Maw-Maw and Paw-Paw's house, my Aunt Carrie and Aunt Katie were there. These exceptional, loving ladies were my father's sisters. Aunt Carrie was visiting from Chicago, Illinois. Aunt Katie lived there in the house with Maw-Maw. My aunts dressed me for my "big day," what you may call my home going. I remember this day like it was yesterday. I wore a white blouse and a red plaid skirt. I sat on the front porch step; waiting in the same place my mother had left me two years earlier. My mother picked me up and we set off for Hot Springs, Arkansas. From Hot Springs we moved to San Antonio, Texas and then to Omaha, Nebraska. All this moving happened within a years-time frame.

In spite of divorcing, my parents always maintained a great friendship with each other even after marrying other people.

Above: Mama, Daddy, Bettie (6), Jimmy (5) and Cassie (7 months).
Below: *Left* – Mama 1944. *Right* - Me - Rosemary (6).

Above: Maw Maw – Gillie King. My paternal grandmother.

Two

MY FATHER

Above: Daddy at Club Delisa in Chicago in 1956.

My father, Daniel King, Sr. was born in Midnight, Mississippi and raised in Marked Tree, Arkansas. Prior to marrying my mother, my father had two children, Ira King and Eva Mae King. While I was living in Memphis, Tennessee my father, was drafted into the Army. He served our country for a short time during World War II. A few years later, my parents separated and eventually divorced.

In spite of the fact that my parents had separated, Maw-Maw, Paw-Paw and my aunts always kept in contact with our family. After living in Hot Springs, Arkansas we moved to San Antonio, Texas and eventually Omaha, Nebraska. We talked on the phone regularly with our family in Marked Tree and Memphis. I distinctly remember when Aunt Carrie called to tell us that Maw-Maw had died. I may have been six or seven years old. It saddened me greatly when she passed.

The following summer we took a road trip back to Arkansas. After resting a couple of days in Marked Tree, Arkansas, Mama took us to Memphis, where we spent the rest of the summer with Daddy and his "new family". He had four girls and two boys. I remember this very clearly. Mama didn't want to go directly to Daddy's house because he had married someone she was not fond of, so she took us to the home of our uncle, Luther Charles (LC).

Uncle LC was Daddy's baby brother. He took us to daddy's house. When we arrived at Daddy's new home, the children had already been put to bed for the night. That night I saw four little chocolate-colored girls in snow-white pajamas, asleep on a bed of snow-white linens. They were so beautiful to me. The next day when we all first met each other, there was love and a real connection. My father said to us all, "There are no half-brothers or half-sisters. And there are no stepbrothers or stepsisters. You are sisters and brothers!" Years later at my oldest sister's funeral, my brother Charles reminded us of this visit and Daddy's words. People were whispering that they didn't know she had so many siblings. From that day until today, we have always been simply brothers and sisters; nothing less.

Above: Daddy at Shepard HS vs Richard HS football 1976.

Eventually my father moved to Chicago, Illinois to be near his sister, Carrie and found employment downtown Chicago at Union train station. When I moved to Chicago in 1960, as a single mother with my two sons, my father became a critical part of my support system and helped me to raise my family. Daddy may not have been in everyone's life 24/7 while we all were growing up, but he always loved and supported us to the best of his ability. According to my children, my father (aka Papa Dan) was the best grandfather EVER! He loved them and they adored him.

When my father moved to Chicago, he took a position as a janitor at Union Station. This was the hub railroad station for all trains leading into downtown Chicago. Daddy always met interesting people on his job but I think his favorite pass time was watching and entertaining the ladies.

If you had met my father on the street going to work, you would have thought he was a businessman going to a high-rise office building. He wore a suit, a starched dress shirt and carried a briefcase. I guess you could say he was a businessman because he was about the business of keeping the station clean. My father was an immaculate man with his body and home. His toilets always passed the "White Glove Test." Because my father worked at Union Station, it was very common to go to Chicago for the summer and Daddy would meet us when we stepped off the train. He would gather up our luggage, hail a cab and send us on our way to Aunt Carrie's home. I'm positive he was the official greeter for all our family members who took the train to Chicago.

Daddy worked as a janitor for over 20 years. He was a member of the union and worked closely with the leaders of the union. The union members were the first to know when job openings were posted. So, when the position of ticket-taker surfaced, the union encouraged him to apply for the position. Daddy was selected and promoted from janitor to ticket taker. He worked in his new position as a ticket taker until he retired many years later.

Daddy's New Family

Above: *Top Left* – Najmah Woods formerly known as Carrie Mae. *Center* – Novella. *Right* – Lois and her husband Charles. **Bottom:** *Left* – Diane. *Right* – Walter Charles. Not pictured is Carl Dennis.

Above*:* *Top* - Eva Mae – Daddy's first born. ***Bottom* – Sisters. Me, Novella, Lois and Eva Mae.

THREE

FINDING HOME IN OMAHA

My grandmother, Cornelius Jackson (aka Little Mama), met and married a soldier named David Jackson. They used his military benefits (the GI bill) to purchase a house built on the hill of 27th Avenue North in Omaha, Nebraska. This is the home where I grew up.

Not long after Little Mama moved to Omaha, she came to visit our home in San Antonio, Texas, where Mama, Bettie (my older sister), Jimmy (my brother), Cassie (my younger sister) and I lived. She came offering a place for her grandchildren to live instead of the small rental house we currently lived in. This house was so small that the only place for the children's bedroom was an enclosed front porch. Our little house was about a block away from the train depot in San Antonio, Texas.

During this time of our lives, my sisters, my brother and I more or less took care of ourselves while Mama and Aunt Georgetta made lunches and sold them to the soldiers assigned to Fort Sam Houston Army Base. My mother and Aunt Georgetta also sold meals to the Negro soldiers who had no restaurant options when the train stopped in San Antonio because of segregation and racism.

Aunt Georgetta was a cousin through marriage. She was the cousin of Aunt Katie's first husband. That is how Aunt Georgetta and Mama met. They became lifelong friends. Aunt Georgetta had one daughter Beatrice (Bea), whose age was between Cassie and I.

When Little Mama arrived in Texas, a hurricane had just blown through and our neighborhood was flooded. Little Mama's timing was perfect because

Mama took her up on her offer to give us a better life in Omaha, Nebraska. While Mama and Aunt Georgetta, finalized their business in Texas, Little Mama returned to Omaha with Cassie. Not long after Little Mama's departure, Mama, Bettie, Jimmy, Aunt Georgetta, Beatrice and I packed up and moved to Omaha.

After we arrived in Omaha, Little Mama began making improvements to the house. She had the gray brick siding removed and replaced it with a stucco finish. The front porch was removed and semicircle stairs took its place. The back porch was closed in with beveled windows and became a guest room. This was phase one of the improvements on the house. Little Mama also worked and established her dressmaking business during this time.

After the outside was completed and paid for, she started on the inside. One of the major changes to the layout of the house was that Little Mama had her kitchen moved to the basement. The old kitchen became her sewing room.

As a natural businesswoman, Little Mama redesigned her spacious home to accommodate live-in boarders. This area of her home was affectionately called "The Hidden Inn". I think she created the first Air Bed and Breakfast.

A spacious family-style room with a large bar was the focal point that greeted everyone when they entered Little Mama's home on the ground floor. A counter divided the kitchen from the dining room. Behind the bar were two bedrooms and behind the kitchen were two more rooms, one was the pantry and the other the laundry room which had a shower and toilet.

In Omaha, at that time, there were lots of Mulberry and Crab Apple trees throughout the community. We had two or three in our yard. One of the enterprising ideas hatched by Little Mama and Mama was that they decided to make two types of wine, Mulberry and Crab Apple wine. After preparing the wine, Mama and Little Mama put the wine in crock-pots, covered them, and placed them on the ledge that was adjacent to the stairs leading into the basement.

This "wine" fermented for about two months. Early one morning about 2 or 3 o'clock in the morning, a massive explosion awakened everyone in the house. We thought the furnace had exploded. Daddy Ted (Little Mama's husband) went downstairs to see what had happened. Upon his return, he made this statement: "Connie, Virdell, let this be the last time the two of you make any wine!" The crock-pots had burst, and wine had run everywhere. Needless to say, everyone pitched in to clean up the mess. After that, the ledge storage area became the stage for the "Annual Christmas Scene."

Above: *Left* - Little Mama's house in Omaha. *Center* – Bettie, Cousin Jessie Louise and me. *Right* – Daddy Ted. **Below:** Christmas Scene on "The Ledge" Little Mama's home.

Below: Wedding Reception in Little Mama's yard. **Backrow:** Me, Bettie, Cynthia in Beatrice's arm, Billy in Uncle T's arms. Mama is in the center holding Norris. Standing behind Mama is William (WT) Anderson, Bettie's husband. **Sitting on the Right Side**: Daddy Ted is holding Teddy. Little Mama is standing to the right of Daddy Ted and Cassie is sitting in front of Little Mama.

Above: *Top* - Mother's Day 1981. *Seated* – Little Mama, Cassie, Billy and Emerald. *Standing* – Dennis, Bettie, Carmela, Carlette, and Mama. *Backrow Standing* - Teddy and Cynthia. **Bottom Photo:** *Standing* – Rodney, Cassie, Bettie. *Seated* - Jimmy, Mama and Little Mama.

LEFT PAGE: *Top Row -* Bettie High School Senior. Bettie (1989). Jimmy U. S. Navy (1962). *Middle Row* – Paul & Jimmy King (1984). Little Sue, Jimmy, Sonja and Dannie (1978). Me (1994). *Bottom Row* – Me (1993), Cassie (1996) and Cassie (1971).

Above: Jimmy, Cassie, Bettie and Me in Omaha Fall 1995.

FOUR

EASTER

The routine on Easter Sunday was this . . . You wore last year's outfit to church in the morning and saved the new Easter outfit for the evening gathering and performance of the Easter Program.

Every year we received a fancy Easter basket full of candy, stuffed animals and other trinkets wrapped in a special rainbow-colored cellophane paper. We were supposed to carry it with us to church and we were supposed to hold it and show it off. But we could not open it until we got back home.

Finally considered a young lady at the age of eight or nine, I was allowed to wear a pair of navy-blue, sling back shoes with a bow on the toe. I adored these shoes! I especially liked the clicking sound the shoes made. They sounded like Mama's high-heeled shoes when she walked . . . "Click. Clack. Click. Clack." While walking home from church that Easter Sunday, I made that clicking sound all the way home.

Apparently, I was a little rough on my shoes; working extra hard to imitate that grown-up rhythmic click-clacking sound because one of the bows came off my new shoe. I dreaded facing my mother because I knew I was in trouble. This was the first time I wore these shoes and I knew Mama would be furious that I had damaged the shoes. Little Mama and her dynamic sewing machine came to the rescue and repaired my shoe just in time for the Sunday evening service that would feature our Easter Pageant. Little Mama reminded me that "Ladies" do not walk click clack down the street.

Above: *Left* - Me (6) Easter Sunday. *Center* – Me (10) and Benny Easter Sunday.
Right – Bettie and Cassie Easter Sunday.
Below*:* Bettie, Cousin Bea, Cassie, Me and Jimmy on Easter Sunday.

That afternoon after returning from church, we finally were able to take the fancy wrapping off the baskets and hunt for eggs. Little Mama had died the

Easter eggs and they were all hidden in the yard. After the Easter egg hunt, we would then go in the house, take our fancy clothes off, and get ready for the big family Easter meal. After we ate it was time to wash dishes and clean up the kitchen. Once the kitchen was cleaned, we needed to get ready for the Easter Pageant. We quickly changed into our new Easter outfits and headed back to church.

By the time we arrived back at the church, all the kids would be lined up and curious to see our fancy dresses as well as the petty coats that Little Mama was famous for making. We were always a hit! The other kids had on store-bought clothes. Our Easter outfits were fancier, more creative, and expertly sewn. Finally, we were ready to perform our annual Easter Program. All the kids had a part orchestrated by our Sunday School Teacher. Most of the time, we each said a poem.

For some reason, I remember one of Cassie's Easter poems: "What are you looking at me for? I didn't come here to stay. I just came to tell you Happy Easter Day!" During our program, we would also sing Easter songs. Sometimes the older kids would perform a skit. The Easter Pageant didn't last more than an hour and a half, but we enjoyed every minute of wearing our new Easter outfits. Soon after, it was time to head home. Easter was finally over.

Above: Me and Daddy Ted on Easter Sunday. I was 13 years old.

FIVE

A ROAD TRIP TO REMEMBER

I remember our first road trip back to Arkansas after having moved to Omaha. All the children were very excited about taking a road trip. Mr. Ted, Little Mama's new husband and my step-grandfather, bought a car for the family. It was a dark gray four-door Pontiac sedan. There was a total of seven passengers on this trip; three adult women and four children.

My mother packed our clothes in a standard size "footlocker" trunk which was placed in the trunk of the vehicle. Mama had a three-piece Samsonite luggage set. Miss Gladys, a family friend and one of Little Mama's boarders, had two or three pieces of luggage. My grandmother, Little Mama, had a very expensive three-piece set of luggage. The three adult women sat in the front seat.

As my mother was packing the car, Little Mama stated, "My luggage cannot go in the trunk because I paid too much money for it." As a result, Little Mama's luggage was placed in the back seat of the car. Several pieces were placed on the floor of the back seat and Cassie and I sat on top of one piece of luggage that was covered with a towel on the back seat. Our feet rested on the luggage stacked on the floor. This road trip was taken long before seatbelt laws.

It was June and Mama dressed Cassie and I in the outfits that Daddy had sent us as Christmas gifts. They were yellow turtleneck shirts with "Rudolph the Red Nose Reindeer" on the front and navy-blue wool pants. The car had no air conditioner and my mother could not drive with the windows down—it made too much noise. It's a wonder we didn't faint. Packed in the car like sardines,

Cassie and I were sweating and our little legs wouldn't stop itching. Ever so often, someone would yell, "Be still, quit wiggling." We were miserable and could not help moving around because of the heat, wool clothing and riding on the top of slippery suitcases.

Traveling on the roads during this time in our country's history was challenging because of "Jim Crow Laws" that prohibited where we could stop, eat or sleep. It is for these reasons that our Aunt Hazel, Uncle Jesse's wife, had packed us lunch and dinner. We stopped at picnic areas for lunch and dinner that we believed were safe for Blacks. Often, we went to the bathroom at the gas stations. There weren't many restaurants or hotels available to Blacks traveling on the road.

Little Mama was the navigator on this trip and was responsible for giving directions. Just outside the city limits of St. Louis, Missouri we saw a sign that read "By-Pass St. Louis". Not understanding the purpose of a by-pass, Little Mama said, "We don't want to bypass St. Louis. We want to go through St. Louis." So, we took the other route that we believed would lead us to St. Louis.

After riding all day Sunday and Sunday night, Mama decided to pull over and get some sleep. We were finally allowed to sleep too. Mama felt it was important that we remained awake and take in the sights of the city and state we were driving through. They wouldn't let us sleep while they were driving. We finally arrived in Marked Tree, Arkansas, on Monday morning at Aunt Virginia and Uncle Charlie's house. Aunt Virginia was Little Mama's oldest sister. Talking to my mother, Uncle Charlie, asked, "Baby, what took you so long to get here?" Little Mama answered . . . "We kept seeing signs that said, By-Pass St. Louis, so we went the other way." Uncle Charlie laughed. "Had you followed the 'Bypass' route, you could have saved time." My Uncle Charlie was a driver for International Harvester, delivering trucks and other equipment so he was much more educated about the highways than my mother and grandmother.

My Aunt Virginia was a loving Southern lady. She was beautiful and lived a very comfortable life. Her complexion was golden brown and her straight dark brown hair accented her petite features. Little Mama and Aunt Virginia's parents were biracial. As a matter of fact, Aunt Virginia's mother is purported to have had red hair. Another thing about my sweet aunt is that she was very pampered. She had a cook and a cleaning lady. Aunt Virginia and Uncle Charlie lived very comfortable lives in a nice home. In addition, they are the ones that raised my mother when my grandmother (Little Mama) wasn't able to raise her.

Needless to say, I could go on and on with stories about Little Mama. Each one is better than the other one.

Above: *Left* – Little Mama and her first car. *Right* – Little Mama, Mama and Ms. Thelma.

Above: *Top* – Aunt Virginia (Ida) Nunn and Uncle Charlie Nunn.

Bottom: *Left* – Aunt Virginia (Little Mama's Sister). *Right* – Uncle Charlie Nunn.

Six

Dreams and Aspirations

Above: Me – Eighth Grade Graduation from Webster Grade School in 1956.

Towards the end of eighth grade, as I was nearing graduation, I began to dream of my future. I aspired to be an accomplished musician. My first dream was to play the piano and continue developing my skills with my violin. My second dream was to become a nurse or a schoolteacher. My third dream was to travel to South Africa and explore that beautiful country. What has amazed me about my dreams and aspirations, is how God chose to fulfill my dreams and aspirations.

During the ages of 13 through 16, I was very active with school and church activities. Unlike much of the nation, schools in Nebraska were integrated, which allowed me to participate in lots of activities. I began piano lessons for 50 cents per class. As I progressed, I began to play the beginning level of classical music. My family didn't exactly support my musical development. Too often, someone would yell out from the other room, "Get off that piano! What you are playing doesn't sound like what Doretha plays." Doretha was the daughter of the pastor of our church. She was the same age as I but had been taking lessons from the age of eight or nine and probably from someone at church. The music Doretha played was mostly organ and church music; which was not of the classical genre. Even though I received little encouragement when I practiced or played, I was not discouraged and maintained my dream to become an accomplished musician.

In addition to playing the piano, I started playing the violin. Often times I hid in my room to practice the violin so that I would not disturb my family. On many occasions I would receive criticism from family members about playing the violin too. My step grandfather (Daddy Ted) once stated, "Who ever heard of a Black violinist?" In spite of the criticism, I became a member of the citywide orchestra for intermediate school students. Usually, the only person who attended my concerts was my brother or sister who walked with me to Joslin Museum, which is where our concerts were held.

At church, it was different. We had a small orchestra at church, which provided music for Sunday school and it is here that my family was able to hear me play. My mother seldom was able to see me in concert with the citywide orchestra because of work and other commitments. As a mother, I attended almost all of my children's concerts, plays and events. I have always been their biggest supporter and cheerleader.

It is obvious that the musical gene was in my body and I passed it on to my children. Each of my children played a musical instrument. Moreover, three of my six children have been blessed with beautiful singing voices. My musical gene and love for the performing arts has been passed down to my children, my grandchildren and my great grandchildren. Besides playing instruments, my children and many of my grandchildren also performed in Readers Theater and Drama receiving many awards and accolades. It has always given me great joy and filled me with so much pride watching my children and grandchildren perform in the performing arts world.

My dreams and aspirations were deferred in 1958 when I became pregnant at the age of 16 with my first child. I was 17 when my first child was born. My mother told me that I could not go back to school after the baby was born. I had to get a job. I kept two babies (my child and my sister's child) during the day and worked the second shift leaving my child at a babysitter. It is very difficult to continue the path of achieving your dreams and aspirations when you make personal choices that are not in alignment with achieving your goals. There were many consequences to becoming a single teenage mother, some good and some bad.

Fifteen months after having my first child, I gave birth to my second child. and my mother informed me that I could no longer stay in her home. It was time for me to be responsible for my two children and myself. This was devastating to me! I truly believed my life was over. Little did I know at that time, that moving in with Aunt Carrie and Uncle Sam would be the best thing that could have happened to me. Aunt Carrie and Uncle Sam were the sister and brother-in-law of my father, Daniel King. Aunt Carrie not only saved my life but she changed its direction.

As a result of motherhood becoming my number one priority, I had to put my educational dreams on hold. I did not receive my High School diploma until I was 26. Five of my six children were present at my High School graduation in 1967 and I was seven months pregnant with L'Tonya. Over the years, I continued my education and in 1986 I graduated with an Associate Degree from Chicago Citywide College. Even though I never became a nurse or schoolteacher, two of my children have been professors at the university level. Furthermore, four of my six children have Bachelor of Science Degrees and two of my six children have Master's Degrees. Even though two of my children never completed formal degree plans at the university level, they both have completed college courses and they are two of the most self-taught and "well-read" people I know. Both are highly intelligent and their knowledge is sought by peers and subordinates on and off the job. When I look at my children's educational achievements, I realize that my dreams and aspirations did not go unfulfilled; they were simply deferred. My children's successes are my successes! They are my legacy.

Moving to Chicago, Illinois in 1960 was the start of my individual growth and in some ways the beginning of my travels as an adult. In the 8th grade I dreamed of going to South Africa and seeing the beauty of that country. While I have not made it to South Africa, I have had lots of travel experiences. Of the 50 United States, I have been to or traveled through 39 states, which includes Alaska. I have had the pleasure of also vacationing in Germany, France, Italy, Spain and Austria. My children are the ones that gifted me with the ability to travel around the United States and overseas to Europe. Four of my six children served in the United States Army and almost every place they served, I visited.

One of my daughters has traveled to Africa three times and through her travels, I have visited the motherland and seen its beauty through her eyes.

When I look back on the dreams and aspirations I had as a child, I now realize that the dreams that God placed in my heart weren't just my dreams but were the dreams and aspirations for my entire family.

Above: *Left* – Me High School 1958. *Right* – Me College Graduation 1985.

Above: My granddaughter, Alicia Allen recently received her Bachelor of Arts degree from American Musical and Dramatic Academy (AMDA) in Los Angeles, California. *Left* - Alicia with her cello. *Right* – Alicia in the recording studio.

SEVEN

HOW MAMA BECAME A MINISTER'S WIFE

Above: Reverend and Mrs. Willie Stile Crawford in 1960.

Our church, Salem Baptist Missionary Church, was having a fall revival in 1959. The guest minister was Reverend W. (Willie) Stile Crawford from

Okmulgee, Oklahoma, which is the county seat of Okmulgee County, Oklahoma. Okmulgee is 38 miles south of Tulsa and 13 miles north of Henryetta via US-75. Mama was a member of the Ushers Board and was serving that night at the revival. She was very attentive to all the people in attendance. My mother has a welcoming and beautiful smile that would make everyone feel comfortable and at ease.

The guest speaker, Reverend Crawford was sitting in the pulpit waiting for the choir to finish singing when he first noticed my mother. He was captivated by Mama's beauty and enjoyed watching her go about her duties as an usher. Later, after he finished preaching his sermon, Rev. Crawford asked our pastor, Rev. J.C. Wade, Sr. who she was because he liked the way she looked and the confidence she exuded. He asked her name and inquired as to whether she was married. It was "love at first sight." Willie (W. Stile) and Willie (Willie Virdell) had a small wedding ceremony in our living room on April 9, 1960. After the wedding, Mama moved to Oklahoma to live with her new husband.

My stepfather, Rev. Crawford, absolutely adored my mother. He spoiled her rotten. His pet name for my mother was "Precious" and he treated her like a precious gem. My mother was warmly welcomed into her new husband's family and his church. They loved and accepted her with open hearts and arms. When they married, Rev. Crawford was the Assistant Pastor of Paradise Baptist Church in Oklahoma City, Oklahoma. Years later he pastured the East Side Baptist Church; in Okmulgee, Oklahoma. Mama absolutely loved being the "First Lady" of his churches. Their marriage was filled with love and they remained married until his death decades later.

Above: *Left* - Rev. W. Stile Crawford. *Right* – Mrs. Virdell Crawford (Mama).

EIGHT

MY GRANDMOTHER AKA LITTLE MAMA

My maternal grandmother, Cornelius Jackson, was the fourth daughter and the fifth child of Will and Bettie Jackson. She was born March 25, 1900. Please don't tell anyone the year she was born, as it was a great family secret. She did not want people to know her age. Will and Bettie Jackson had nine children but only five lived to be adults.

I never heard anything about her early childhood. One of her most prominent features was that she was a very petite woman; standing only 4 feet 8 inches tall and weighed only 89 lbs. She was so petite that she was lovingly called "Little Mama". Her skin was caramel-colored and she had jet-black hair.

Cornelius's father, Will Jackson, was a bi-racial man whose father (Master Parks) was a white plantation owner in Goldsboro, North Carolina. Will's mother was one of Master Park's slaves. Cornelius' mother, Bettie Jackson, was also bi-racial. She was described as a redheaded Irish woman. After Will and Bettie married, they went west to Arkansas.

I was named after my grandmother Cornelius Jackson. Even though everyone knew my grandmother as Little Mama; she was only small in her stature. She was not little in her love for her family or her determination to do what she felt was right. Little Mama was an excellent seamstress. She could make just about anything, with a pattern or without. As a gifted seamstress, she expertly made clothing, coats and hats. With great pride and perfection, she completed her work and expected the same from us.

One year I took a Home Economics class in school. I made a blouse in this class and received a grade of "B" on this project. I was very proud of my work and grade. I brought it home and showed it to Little Mama. She said, "That's nice, but this is wrong and that is wrong." She started ripping my blouse apart. I said, "Little Mama, I have to wear that blouse tomorrow; it's part of my grade." Her reply was, "You will." I spent the next two hours working on my blouse. Little Mama ensured that I completed my blouse to her satisfaction and standards. As required, the next day I wore my new and improved blouse to school. My teacher was so impressed with my work that my grade jumped up to "A+." In those few hours, Little Mama taught me much about workmanship.

I quickly became an expert seamstress just like Mama and Little Mama. I made the majority of my own clothes, most of my children's clothing as well as prom and wedding dresses. In addition to sewing for my family, I also made the cannon cover for Prairie View A&M University's ROTC program and many costumes and props for Salyards Middle School's Theater department.

Above: *Left*– Little Mama, Me and Mama at Wedding 1984. *Right* – Cassie, Little Mama and Mama on Mother's Day 1983.

Above: Annual Formal Ball 1955 - Mama, Little Mama and Miss Glades.

In addition to teaching me so much about being an expert seamstress and tailor, it was Little Mama who taught me that I was beautiful just the way I was. She loved my complexion and taught me to love my complexion too. As I stated earlier, I have the same dark complexion as my father and because of this, I was sometimes called "Old Black May". Little Mama gave me this reply to anyone that called me "Old Black May" . . . . I would say "I would rather be black than that shitty color you are!" That stopped the name-calling. Little Mama was my Champion and savior.

Little Mama and I could talk about anything. To me, she was endearing because of her many different characteristics. She was very secretive. There were many things that she didn't want people to know about her. For example, she dyed her hair even though she usually wore a wig. In addition, she had little to no bust or hips and wore padded bras and padded panties for the illusion of seductive curves. She also had false teeth. To me, as a child, these things were not "bad" for people to know. She truly did not want us to give away her secrets. Even with her many secrets, I thought Little Mama was beautiful.

My grandmother wasn't just a beautiful person who loved beautiful things; she was also a very classy lady. She lived a very colorful life and was a skilled seamstress.

One of the things I remember most about Little Mama was the funny things she often said. Every time she cooked roast beef she would ask her husband, "Ted Jones, do you know how much this roast cost?" Daddy Ted would reply, "No, Connie, what did it cost?" And she would say, "It cost 59 cents a pound." Then Daddy Ted would reply with his standard answer, "Worth every penny! Worth every penny!" This conversation was repeated every time that Daddy Ted failed to compliment her in a timely manner on the dinner she had prepared.

NINE

LITTLE MAMA – THE SPICE OF LIFE

Little Mama was an exciting, adventurous and a very colorful young woman. She lived with many secrets and I only know of a few of her secrets. I'm certain she had more. I learned about this story from my other favorite relative, Aunt Carrie, my father's youngest sister. Aunt Carrie made it very clear to me that this is a family secret that has been well guarded.

One summer after moving to Chicago, I became the designated driver for my grandmother and mother on a road trip to North Carolina. They were headed there for the "Jackson Family Reunion". I became their designated chauffeur because my sister, Cassie, their usual cross-country driver, had gotten sick and could not drive them that far. So, the plan was that Cassie would drive them to Chicago and stay at my house with my children, and I would take them the rest of the way to North Carolina.

While riding through the countryside, Little Mama would say things like, "This town has really grown." My mother responded with, "you've never been here before." Little Mama would reply, "Yes, I have." What was strange to me was that my mother never asked when Little Mama had been through this part of the country. It was apparent to me that they had an unspoken "code," which was between them and for no one else to know. The other unspoken lesson to me was . . . never asked any questions.

When I got back home, Aunt Carrie asked me how the trip went and I told her how Little Mama was always talking about how the country had grown like she had been there before. This is when Aunt Carrie informed me of one of the well-guarded family secrets about Little Mama. I was practically sworn to secrecy.

As the story goes, Cornelius Jackson Jones, AKA Connie, AKA Little Mama had lived a very colorful life in the 1920s and '30s (prohibition times). Not only did she ride with whiskey runners but also, she was arrested by the "Feds" and imprisoned. I was never told exactly how she became involved with moonshiners, but over the years, I've gotten a little of the background story.

One of the first things I learned was that Little Mama's sister, Mary Blackman, was a businesswoman in Parkman, Arkansas. She had rent houses, a small neighborhood store, a cafe, and shall we say a "small motel" where men rented rooms by the hour. All of her businesses were located in a cul-de-sac. My Great Aunt Mary's home was a large house at the beginning of the street. Aunt Mary was much older than Little Mama and had two children about the same age as Little Mama. Unfortunately, both of Aunt Mary's children died under questionable circumstances.

I suspect that Aunt Mary and her family, along with Little Mama, were involved with the whiskey runners. More than likely, the whiskey runners probably spent some time at the "motel" where they met a young Cornelius (Connie) Jackson who was stunning. Not only was she beautiful, but she was also very intelligent. These characteristics were probably what sparked their interest in Cornelius Jackson.

Most likely, these gentlemen invited her to travel along with them to the East Coast. As you will remember, Little Mama was very familiar with the countryside when I drove her and Mama to the Jackson Family Reunion. Her comments indicated that she had traveled through those areas and knew the region well. I feel confident that Little Mama learned her business skills from her sister and some from the mobsters. While I do not know what her role was with the whiskey runners or mobsters, we do know that she was caught and prosecuted.

Above: *Left* – Cornelius Jackson (aka Little Mama). *Right* – Virdell King (Mama) and Little Mama in Hot Springs, Arkansas about 1944.

In the end, she was caught by the "Feds." I want to think it was Elliot Ness who caught her. She spent around five years in the penitentiary. The fact that Little Mama spent years running with the whiskey runners and five years in the federal penitentiary is most likely the reason Aunt Virginia and Uncle Charlie raised my mother. During the time that Little Mama was incarcerated, she learned the trade of sewing, which brought her a good income when she was released.

Many years later during my weekly phone visits with my sister Bettie, she told me about Little Mama's "Federal Vacation." My reply was, "I've known about that for a long time." Bettie said, "But you didn't tell me!" I responded,

"I was told this was a family secret and not to say anything to anyone." "Who told you?" Bettie asked. "Aunt Carrie." I replied. Finally, my sister Bettie said, "Well, you sure can keep a secret."

In addition to the sewing skills both my mother and grandmother possessed, they were also innovative. Once, Little Mama and Mama decided to shorten the legs on a wrought iron bed. They wanted to make the bed look more modern. After much thought and planning, they took the legs to the hardware store and the worker shortened the legs. By shortening the legs, they were able to achieve their desired effect. The bed looked more modern and was also easier to access.

As I stated earlier, my mother and grandmother were very innovative. They were constantly thinking of creative things to do. One day while Little Mama and Mama were out shopping, they purchased an apple tree. When they returned home, Daddy Ted dug a hole in our backyard for the tree. While he was digging the hole, Mama and Little Mama were busy tying freshly grown apples to the tree's branches. The neighborhood children were busy playing their evening "baseball game," so they were not paying attention to what the grownups were doing. After the game ended, Mama called everyone over to where they had planted the tree and told everyone to pick an apple from the new tree. All the children picked an apple from this freshly planted tree and ate it. If anyone ever suspected that these apples did not grow on that tree, no one said a word. I don't know if the tree ever started bearing fruit, but when I left home at the age of 18, the tree had not produced a single apple.

Even though I lived in a home with many rules, some were very stringent, some very straightforward, while others you just had to figure out on your own, there were many happy and fun times in our home too. I could go on and on about some of the things that my mother and grandmother did that made our lives fun and interesting. They were true innovators and lived life to its fullest.

Above: Aunt Mary Blackman, Little Mama's sister.

TEN

MY KEEPSAKES

My most precious keepsakes are a vanity tray bequeathed to me from Little Mama. The mirrored tray is about 18 inches long and has two clear ornate perfume bottles. In addition, after my mother died, I received the tray and a beautiful crystal lamp that Little Mama promised me. I am sure it has monetary value because when the tray's mirror broke and I took the mirror in for repair, the shop owner wanted to buy it. When I look at this tray, I remember "Little Mama" very fondly. She loved beautiful things and had a lot of them.

These items that once belonged to Little Mama are items that I truly cherish. I am so thankful for the heritage that has been handed down to me. I'm blessed that I had time with my grandmother and that I had the opportunity to learn from her and to come to know what was important to her. Looking at Little Mama's personal items reminds me daily of her and the glamorous life she lived. To me, in a way, Little Mama is still here with me.

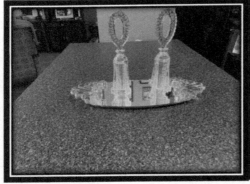

Above: *Top* – Crystal Lamp.
Bottom: *Left* – Crystal Vanity Set. *Right* – Little Mama's Watch. All items bequeath to me by Little Mama.

Eleven

LOCKHART ACADEMY

When I moved to Chicago, Illinois with my two sons, we moved in with my father's sister Carrie. My aunt, Carrie Ruth Lockhart, quickly became invaluable to me. She is the reason that I became a responsible parent and an accountable adult. Aunt Carrie taught me what it takes to be a survivor. She taught me that I was somebody, and she taught me how to feel good about myself. In many ways her lessons were taught to me by her living example. I learned to love myself.

My paternal grandmother (Gillie King aka Maw Maw), who I stayed with in Memphis, Tennessee, when I was two years old is Aunt Carrie's mother. Maw Maw had five children and Aunt Carrie was her third child. She grew up in Marked Tree, Arkansas with her other siblings. Maw Maw had been married previously and had two children from that marriage, Katie (Aunt Katie) and Talbert (known as Uncle Son). A few years later after her husband died, Maw Maw married my grandfather Walter King (aka Paw Paw). Of this marriage, Maw Maw and Paw Paw had three children, Carrie, Daniel (my father) and Luther Charles.

Aunt Carrie's first husband was Mr. James Young, who died at a young age. He was the father of my Aunt Carrie's only son James Charles (known as JC). JC had two children, Regina and Norman. Years after having been widowed, Aunt Carrie and Uncle Sam met in Memphis, Tennessee and started dating. Before Uncle Sam left to serve his country during World War II, they were married. After the war, Aunt Carrie and Uncle Sam moved to Chicago and resided on the south side of the city. Uncle Sam was able to find employment as a Pullman Porter with the Burlington Railroad. He was a porter on the Burlington Zephyr train that ran from New York to California. This train was famous for making its "Dawn-to-Dusk" run between Denver and Chicago, which broke the record for nonstop train travel and speed during that time. Uncle Sam worked as a Pullman Porter until his death in 1963.

When I went to live with Aunt Carrie, she lived in a two-bedroom apartment on 59th street. My children and I occupied the back bedroom. When my oldest daughter was born, she actually slept in the top drawer of the chest of drawers in our room. Aunt Carrie was the type of person that tried to help everyone who came her way. You could earn points with her by maintaining good behavior or not repeating wrong behavior. In addition, she was an excellent listener and motivator. She truly wanted all young people in the family to be successful. This is why she gladly opened her home to my children and me.

Carrie Lockhart was always well put together. Before wigs became popular, she got up and curled her hair and put her make-up on every morning. She never went anywhere without earrings and usually a necklace. It was important to her to create the perfect appearance even before she cooked breakfast and greeted the family.

Aunt Carrie and Uncle Sam had a routine. When Uncle Sam would return from his train runs which usually lasted between 3 to 7 days, the first thing he would do is stop at the bank and cash his check. Then he would stop at the grocery store and shop for his favorite breakfast, which consisted of dinner rolls, rice, sausage, scrambled eggs, and coffee. Aunt Carrie would cook his favorite breakfast while he took a shower and cleaned up. Next, they would sit together and pay their bills. This was their routine when Uncle Sam returned from work.

Uncle Sam loved children and was very good to Regina, Norris, Kelly, and Carol. He wasn't a church-going man, but he supported the church that Aunt Carrie attended. -Aunt Carrie decided as an adult that she would learn to play the piano. So, she bought a piano and took lessons, and became the only musician for the church. I was impressed that as an adult she decided to learn to play the piano, and then achieved her goal. Her actions inspired me to return to school and accomplish my own personal goals too.

One of the funniest things that happened when we lived with Aunt Carrie was that she would often sit on her couch and look out the window. She would watch the cars driving by and the people walking by her building. My sons Norris and Kelly would often sit with her as she looked out the window. Often when she would see a particular tenants from her building entering their apartment building Aunt Carrie would say, "Here comes Mr. Bastard." One day, while sitting with Aunt Carrie and looking out the window, Norris told Kelly, "There goes a blue bastard." Then Kelly said, "There's a green one." Stunned by what I heard my four- and three-year-old sons say, I asked them, "Why did you say that?" Norris replied, "Because there is one, see!" while pointing to one of the cars driving down the street. I was relieved that they were not talking about people and I quickly explained to them that those things are called cars. Both Aunt Carrie and I learned a valuable lesson about being mindful of "little ears" living in our home.

Carrie Lockhart was the "Dean" of Lockhart Academy and her sister, Katie White, was one of the instructors. Aunt Carrie understood the hardship of my childhood, the circumstances I was currently living in and the parenting skills I needed to be a successful mother. She provided me first with the tools I needed to forgive. Then she taught me how to let go of the past and move forward in life. I needed all these skills in order to be the best mother for my children. I will forever be grateful to Aunt Carrie and Aunt Katie for what they have done for me.

**Above*:* *Top Left* - Aunt Carrie and Aunt Katie. *Top Right* – Aunt Carrie. *Bottom Left* – Steven, Marcus, Norman & Aunt Carrie. *Bottom Right* – Aunt Katie.

Above: *Left* - Aunt Carrie and Reverend Hopkins. ***Right*** – [***From the top to bottom***] Rev. Hopkins, JC, Aunt Carrie, Uncle Son, Sallie and Norman. **Bottom:** *Left* - Aunt Katie 2005. ***Right*** – Aunt Katie White 1995.

Above: Daddy, Me, Carol, Kelly and Norris. Chicago 1962. Lockhart Academy.

MY CHILDREN

Above: King Family at Kelly's Wedding to Glenda in 2000. Marcus, Carol, Me, Kelly, L'Tonya, Steven and Norris.

Below: *Left* – Kelly, Carol and Norris. *Center* – Kelly, Carol, Norris, Steven and L'Tonya. *Right* -Marcus, L'Tonya, Steven and Carol.

Above: My Family at my 70th Surprise Birthday Party.

TWELVE

NORRIS

Above: Norris Dean King, High School Senior Portrait 1977.

Norris, my oldest child, gave me the chance to learn what motherhood was all about. As a curious child, Norris tried many things and often tried your patience too. He has always been very smart and eager to learn. In fact, his intelligence earned him the nicknames of "Brains" and "The Professor". As the oldest of my children, he helped a lot with the day-to-day operations of our home. When Norris was in the fifth or sixth grade, he and Kelly had a paper route. They would get up, get dressed, and load up their wagon with their newspapers. Back then, our family only had one bike, so that is why they had to use a wagon to deliver the morning papers. They would leave around 6:30 am to deliver papers to the back section of Altgeld Gardens. Altgeld Gardens is a public housing project in Chicago that was originally built for the Negro Veterans that returned from World War II in need of housing.

Each day it took Norris and Kelly about 45 minutes to an hour, depending on the weather, to complete their route. They became friends with many of their clients to include the lunchroom ladies who worked at Carver High School. These ladies took a liking to them and gave them a hot cinnamon coffee cake every morning. One day I took some of the children that were part of the free lunch program at Carver Elementary School over to the high school cafeteria. Those nice ladies told me, "There are two little boys that deliver papers here every morning. You should bring them over here for lunch too." I asked the ladies what they looked like. They described them, and I told them, "Those are my boys, and unfortunately they don't qualify." These women spoke very highly of my sons and hearing their words made me very proud of them and their work ethic. That job lasted about six months until their boss decided he didn't want to pay them for their labor. I remember Norris saying, "If you don't pay, I don't work." Even back then, Norris was demonstrating his keen business mind.

After that, the boys got a job delivering telephone books working with their dad. One day it started snowing while they were out delivering phone books. I didn't want the boys' feet to freeze so I headed toward the south side of Chicago in search of my boys. I located them on 56th Street coming out of a building; their poor little feet were soaking wet. I gave them their boots and some dry socks, which they quickly put on. They were so happy to see me and thanked me over and over. Of course, their dad wasn't as pleased; he said I was pampering my boys. I was just trying to be a good mother and I knew my boys would be very grateful for my thoughtfulness.

One day I had to take a friend who was very sick to the emergency room. After arriving at the hospital, I realized that I was going to be at the hospital for a while. I called home and told Norris to get the other kids ready because I was going to take them over to my aunt's house. Norris decided to comb Carol's hair. There was a hair product on the market called Dippity Do that I often used on her hair. It was a gel and I would put it on the edges of Carol's hair. Not really knowing how to comb Carol's hair, Norris decided to put the Dippity Do on her braids. Carol's hair was divided into three braids; one braid on each side and one in the back. Norris was so slow in putting the Dippity Do on her hair that the gel thickened and he couldn't comb her hair. So, Norris decided to cut off the whole braid. When I arrived home to pick them up Carol was crying. I was very upset, but I think Carol was even more upset. In the end, I had to cut her hair more in order to even out her hair. Fortunately, her hair grew back pretty fast. Unfortunately for Norris, he could NOT sit down for a while.

Norris was a great student who was actively engaged in school. He earned As and Bs throughout his school years. In Middle School he played the saxophone and took part in many of the school plays. He played football at the high school level and participated in Readers Theater and Drama. Norris had key roles in almost every play his school produced while he was at Richards High School. He even sang in a couple of the musicals. I really enjoyed attending his performances. It made me very proud to be his mother.

In Norris' senior year of high school, I received a phone call from his school counselor informing me that he would not graduate because he had been skipping school. I did not know Norris was skipping school. Two years earlier, our school district built a new high school (Alan B. Shepard HS) and gave the then eleventh grade students the option to continue attending Richards High School or go to the new school. Norris decided to stayed at his old school and not attend school with his brother and sister. As a result of his choice, I now had three high school students that went to two different schools, catching two different buses. When they left home, Kelly and Carol got on the Shepard HS bus going west, and Norris was supposed to be getting on the Richard HS bus going north. Obviously, Norris was not getting on the bus regularly.

That day when the counselor telephoned to tell me of Norris ditching school, she and I made a deal. Instead of Norris riding the bus to school every morning, I would drive him right up to the school where the counselor was waiting. Each morning I handed my senior (aka Norris King) over to his counselor. This took place every day for two weeks. How embarrassing it must have been for a senior to have his mother bring him to school and hand him over to the counselor. I'm sure it was embarrassing but Norris never said a word. He knew that if he complained the consequences would be even worse. My children knew they had consequences when they acted up in school. In fact, if they choose to act out anywhere, I would act out there too. I took no prisoners. They knew that "Mama was crazy!" and "Mama didn't play!" The solution that the counselor and I came up with was the cure for the "Senior Blues".

Throughout Norris' childhood, he was the trailblazer with his behavior. So it was always important to me that I disciplined Norris with appropriate punishments that would deter the other children from following in his footsteps. Needless to say, I did not have any more "Senior Blues," as I called it in my home. Norris' high school graduation was the only time I cried at one of my children's graduations. I think it was because he was my first child to graduate.

After completing high school, Norris immediately joined the Army and served his time in "Military Intelligence". Norris really enjoyed serving in the

Army. His service inspired both his sisters and my youngest son to also join the Army and serve their country.   Following his service to our nation, Norris decided to become a salesman. There is no doubt in any of our minds that Norris is a gifted salesman and orator. He has earned many awards and accolades in his profession and is capable of selling an Eskimo a refrigerator.

Norris has four children, Blake, Jasmine, Connie and Desiree. He also has nine grandchildren.

Above: Norris and Evada with their grandchildren, Eden, Angelica, Isaac and Makayla.

Above: *Top* – Connie, Desiree, Blake and Jasmine. *Left* – Connie, Desi, Me and Jasmine. *Right* – Norris, Desiree and Evada.

Above: ***Top Left*** – Norris King U.S. Army Basic Training 1977. ***Top Right*** – Norris 2022.

Bottom: ***Left*** – Desiree, Norris, Lavelle, Blake and Jasmine. ***Cente***r – Norris, Connie, Desiree and Jasmine. ***Righ***t – Jacob and Noah.

Above: *Top Left* – Blake and Kamille. *Top Right* – Jasmine – Bachelor's Degree.
Bottom: *Left* - Connie, Noah and Jacob. *Righ*t – Isaac, Desiree, Eden, Angelica and Makayla.

THIRTEEN

KELLY

Above: Kalvin Kelly King High School Senior Portrait 1978.

Kelly is my second child; he came along 15 months after Norris was born. Even though his first name is Kalvin, we have always called him Kelly. His full name is Kalvin Kelly King (KKK). Kelly was a good child, very sweet and loveable.

He was a child that wanted to please you and he always did as he was told. Kelly has always valued relationships and works hard at maintaining them. As Kelly grew older, he took on more responsibilities in regards to helping with the other kids. His loving kindness showed in everything he did.

When Kelly and Norris were school aged and we lived in "The Gardens" I was the Den Mother for their Cub Scout Troop. My den was filled with Norris, Kelly and several of the classmates. As a Den Mother, I developed a special relationship with Kelly and his friends that were in my den. Our den participated in community service projects and was honored to carry the American flag during a centennial parade honoring our city. When Kelly was in the 5th grade, we moved from "The Gardens" to the suburb of Robbins, Illinois in 1971 and we left the den. In 1978 when Kelly was a freshman in college he reunited with two of his Cub Scout brothers. They recognized each other one day walking across campus.

We were reunited with another member of our Cub Scout Troop about 5 years ago. While participating in the "Soft Opening" of a neighborhood restaurant here in Cypress, Texas, I had the pleasure of reuniting with another one of my Cub Scouts from my den. He was walking through his restaurant and greeting the patrons who were present for the "Soft Opening." I overheard him say to another patron that he was from Chicago, Illinois. This statement caught my attention and caused me to take a good look at this young man. I was confident that I knew him. I then asked him if he lived in Altgeld Gardens. My former cub scout, turned to look at me directly and slowly said . . . "Mrs. Major?" Tears instantly welled up in his eyes. He told me later that he had not too long ago buried his mother and seeing me brought back so many sweet childhood memories. He is now a very successful businessman who owns dozens of restaurants and businesses throughout Texas.

At Kerr Middle School Kelly joined the school band and played the saxophone. He quickly learned to read music and play his instrument. Kelly also was in theater in middle school and high school. He played the lead role as Walter Lee in "A Raisin in the Sun" in a high school play and performed magnificently. I was so proud of him. During his high school years, Kelly also played football, wrestled and was on the track & field team as a "shot put" thrower. Year round, Kelly participated in school activities and supported his friends in their activities as well. If there was an event happening at Alan B. Shepard High School, Kelly was there as a member of that organization or was there supporting his closest friends. He was an exceptional student in his academics as well.

Kelly was the perfect big brother. He took pride in taking care of his younger brothers and sisters. His acts were always selfless, putting the welfare of his siblings before himself. Kelly was also the peacemaker amongst my children. He wanted everyone to get along and took extra steps to ensure that they played together peacefully. In addition, Kelly also protected his younger siblings and set a perfect example for them to follow.

Once Kelly earned his driving permit and learned to drive, he became my trusted driver of the family. When I told him to take his siblings to where ever (school or the store), he would do that and come straight back home, unlike his brother Norris. Therefore, Kelly became the designated driver of our family. He was a mature and responsible driver. I never worried when Kelly was placed in charge. I knew he would do exactly as I asked him. In Kelly's senior year of high school, I was admitted in the hospital for two weeks. At this time Carol who was a junior in high school, ran the house and cooked the meals. Kelly was responsible for driving his siblings places to include visiting me at the hospital. He also had a part-time job at a local restaurant where he worked after school. Every morning I'd call him to make sure that they were up and getting ready to go to school. Kelly ensured that everyone got up, got dressed and caught the bus to school. Moreover, he ensured that everyone made it home from school safely each day. My next-door neighbor would check on them in the evenings.

And as an added safety measure, I had a friend that would come over and spend the night with them. With Kelly in charge at home, I could rest peacefully and fully recover from my surgery.

In 1977, when Kelly was a junior at Shepard HS and Norris was a senior at Richard HS. Both of them were on their respective high school football teams. It was Shepard HS's Homecoming Game and they were honoring all the player's fathers. Shepard HS and Richard HS were and still are the biggest rivals. This game literally had brothers playing against brothers just like my sons. My father, Kelly and Norris' grandfather (aka Papa Dan) came to the game to fill in for their father. In an effort to be unbiased, Daddy sat on Shepard's side of the field and wore a Shepard football jersey the first half of the game. During the second half of the game, Daddy changed into a Richard's football jersey and sat on the other side of the field. My father was honored to be the father figure for his grandsons in such a monumental game. *[See Photo in Chapter Two.]*

After Kelly graduated from high school in 1978, he became the first of my children to attend college. I told Kelly that he could attend any public college in the state of Illinois. My children were eligible for the Illinois State Scholarship, which paid for tuition and fees. The PELL Grant and work-study would pay for their room and board. Kelly chose the state college that was the furthest from the Chicago land area, which was Southern Illinois University (SIU) at Carbondale.

Sending a child to college was new to me and required a tremendous amount of paperwork and effort on my part. Kelly majored in Engineering and in his freshman year Kelly quickly made the Dean's List with all As and two Bs. Towards the end of his freshman year, Kelly met and then married Valerie. In his sophomore year Kelly elected to take an internship with Kellogg Company in Omaha, Nebraska in order to support his new family. They were expecting my first grandchild. Some might say that Kelly received his "PhD" in anatomy while at SIU.

Kelly was a trailblazer for his younger siblings. Each younger brother and sister followed in Kelly's footsteps and went off to college after graduating from high school. And each of his younger siblings received at a minimum a Bachelor of Science Degree. I will always be grateful to Kelly for paving the way for his siblings in their educational goals.

Kelly has two children, Kris and Lauren. He has five grandchildren.

Above: Kris, Glenda, Kelly and Karon.

Above: *Top Left* - Kris. *Top Right* - Kelly and Kris.

Bottom: *Left* – Lauren. *Right* - London, Elysia, Lauren, Harold Jr. and Tairyn.

Above: *Top* – Knighton, Kris, London, Karon and Kelly.

Bottom: *Left* - Elysia, London, Tairyn and Harold Jr. *Right* – Lauren.

Above: *Left* – Lauren. *Right* - London, Harold Jr., Tairyn, Lauren and Elysia.

Bottom: *Left* Kris and Kelly. *Center* – Karon. *Right* – Knighton and Kris.

Fourteen

CAROL

Above: Carol Lynett King, High School Senior Portrait 1979.

I was happy when Carol was born because she wasn't a boy. Carol was born on Thursday, November 23, 1961 on Thanksgiving Day. The night before she was born, I was helping my aunt prepare Thanksgiving dinner for the next day. When I realized I was in labor I told Aunt Carrie and she said, "You won't be able to have Thanksgiving dinner." I said, "Oh, yes, I will!" Carol was born at 10:06 am in the morning; later that afternoon I had Thanksgiving dinner at the hospital.

Carol was a beautiful baby. Aunt Carrie said, "This is the kind of baby you don't have to dress in all sorts of frills. She just has natural beauty. So don't put all those fancy frills on her." Aunt Carrie was right she was beautiful in anything she wore.

Carol was a "tomboy" and wanted to do everything her brothers did to include climbing trees, playing baseball and playing in the woods. She loved being outside and hated cooking and doing laundry. On the flip side, she didn't mind cleaning and absolutely loved mowing the yard. The boys didn't have to worry about cutting the yard because Carol always volunteered to cut the grass.

Our town, Robbins had a girls' softball league, which Carol joined in the 6th grade. She played 1st base, 2nd base and pitched. She was a really good player having played baseball and softball with her brothers for years. In the 8th grade Carol joined her Middle School band and "attempted" to play the clarinet. I am convinced that the Band teacher, Mr. Pate, knew she did not have any talent but allowed her to remain in the band. Carol was wise enough to fake like she was playing her instrument, ensuring no sounds came from the clarinet. She quickly learned that music was not her gift and this included singing.

Once Carol was in high school, I insisted that she take typing and shorthand. Because of these skills, Carol never held a job in retail or in food service because she was always able to find employment as a secretary. She was able to pay for many of her college expenses by being a secretary or typing other student's papers. I wanted her to know how to type and take dictation because I knew that she would be able to use these skills throughout life.

While in high school, Carol also was in Readers Theater and Drama. Even though she only received small parts in the school plays, she really enjoyed being in theater. Carol also ran track in high school. She actually ran hurdles and mastered the technique. Two colleges offered her scholarships to run hurdles, which she declined because she did not want to go to college. In her senior year of high school Carol was working downtown Chicago at the Harris Bank as a secretary. Carol was very content with this job but I wanted her to go to college. I kept stressing to Carol the importance of getting a college education but she was not listening. Finally, she and I struck a deal. She would go to college for one year and if she did not like it, she could back home.

In August, just before Carol was scheduled to depart for college, the city of Chicago celebrated its annual Bud Billiken Day Parade. Since 1929, the Bud Billiken Day Parade has celebrated Black American youth and the importance of our youth getting an education. It is a back-to-school celebration that includes a picnic, music and dance. Carol asked me if she could go to the parade and take her sister L'Tonya. I told her yes but they would have to catch the bus back home. One of Carol's friends, Mel Carter and her little brother, Joe would also be going to the parade with Carol and L'Tonya. Years earlier, I had taught all my children how to ride the Chicago Transit System. This was necessary because we only had one car and many times it was necessary for them to travel in and around the city. I was very comfortable with my children riding the bus home from the parade even though it was about 25 miles away and would require them transferring buses four times.

I dropped them off in Chicago at Washington Park, and they were supposed to go on to the parade. Unknown to me, Carol decided that she would go see a friend of hers that lived on the other side of Washington Park. She left L'Tonya, Mel, and Joe at the parade and instructed them to wait for her to return. After the parade was over, Carol had not returned to the park to take the group back home. I learned later that Carol had misjudged the distance from her friend's home and the parade. It was a lot further than she anticipated and the parade was a lot shorter than she thought.

Above: *Top Left* – Carol, Major, U.S. Army. ***Top Right* –** Carol (1996).
Bottom: *Left* – Carol, Garrick and Sydni (2009). ***Right* –** Sydni, Garrick and Carol (2021).

Above: *Top Left* – Sydni HS Senior 2021. *Top Right* – Carol, Garrick and Sydni.
Bottom: *Left* – Lennox, Jason, Perris and Sydni at Disney World 2020. *Right* –
Garrick, Me and Carol PVAMU Military Ball 2006.

Above: Garrick, Alma (Garrick's Mother), Sydni, Carol and Me. European Cruise 2016.

By the grace of God, even though L'Tonya was only in the 6th grade, she knew how to get home utilizing the bus system. L'Tonya, Mel and Joe found their way home safely. This was the summer of 1979, at least a decade before everyone had cell phones so there was no way for us to communicate with each other, while they rode on the buses home.

In the meantime, Carol returned to the park but the park was clear and L'Tonya, Mel and Joe were nowhere to be found. Carol wondered around the park for hours looking for her sister and friends. Realizing she had no choice but to call me and explain the situation, Carol called home. When I answered the phone, Carol asked me, "Is L'Tonya there?" I asked her, "What the hell do you mean is L'Tonya there? She is supposed to be with you." As Carol began to explain what happened, I stopped her and asked what was her location. I told her to not move from that location and that I would be there shortly. I hung up the phone, then called Aunt Carrie and told her of the situation. I then jumped in my car and headed to Chicago. I sped all the way to Chicago and made it to Carol's location in record time. My child was missing and I was furious with Carol for creating this situation.

Once I reached Carol's location, I pulled the car to a screeching halt and Carol got in the car. Keeping my right hand on the steering wheel, I reached over with my left hand and punched Carol in the eye. I was infuriated! My baby daughter was missing. Even though we were actually closer to Aunt Katie's house, I drove to Aunt Carrie's home on 59th Street. I knew Aunt Carrie would know what to do.

When we reached Aunt Carrie's home we immediately went inside. Aunt Carrie took one look at Carol's eye and directed her to go get some frozen vegetables out of the freezer and put them on her eye. Then Aunt Carrie told me to calm down and reminded me that I had taught my children how to navigate the streets of Chicago. She then instructed Carol to call home and see if L'Tonya had made it home. When Carol called our home, Marcus answered the phone and told her that L'Tonya had been home but was now at her friend Sherry's home. Unbeknownst to Carol, Sherry and all her friends were having a surprise going away to college party for Carol that evening. L'Tonya had gone to the party. After speaking with Marcus, Carol called to Sherry's home and spoke directly to L'Tonya who explained that when she (Carol) did not return to the park, she decided to catch the bus home. Once Carol hung up from talking to L'Tonya she explained to Aunt Carrie and I what had happened.

Aunt Carrie snickered and then said, "Something about that Bud Billiken Parade ain't it May?" Her words stopped me dead in my tracks and all the anger I was feeling towards Carol instantly dissolved. Back when I was in high school in 1958, I had come to visit Aunt Carrie in Chicago and had gone to the Bud Billiken Parade and met up with Norris' father. This meeting laid the groundwork for the beginning of Norris.

Carol went to college and graduated from Southern Illinois University with a Bachelor's of Science Degree in Retail Management. She was the first one in my family to receive a college degree. Eventually, Carol followed in Norris' footsteps and joined the Army.

On the day that Carol graduated from the Army's basic training at Fort Jackson, South Carolina, Aunt Carrie and I were walking towards the seating area to watch the graduation. All of a sudden, we heard this very distinctive rich voice and the soldiers responding in cadence. I told Aunt Carrie, "Listen, that sounds like Carol, but I don't see her." Finally, I realized it was Carol leading the soldiers. She had been out in the sun so long that she was dark as I am. I want you to know that my heart swelled till I thought it was going to pop. I was so proud of her. Carol was the "Senior Squad Leader" and was leading her platoon in the graduation ceremony barking out commands. Later, Carol's drill sergeant asked whom we came to visit and I told them, "We came down for my oldest daughter's graduation and that my youngest daughter just arrived to begin basic training today." I was proud of both my daughters.

Norris had explained to Carol that since she already had a degree, she could apply for Officer Candidate School after she finished basic training. Carol was commissioned as a 2nd Lieutenant in the Army in 1988. While serving her country Carol earned a Master's of Science Degree in Logistics Management. She served over 22 years in the U.S. Army and retired as a Lieutenant Colonel.

Carol has one child, Sydni.

FIFTEEN

MARCUS

Above: Marcus Newton Major, High School Portrait 1981.

When Marcus was born, he joined Norris, Kelly, and Carol in our tiny little three-room apartment over a storefront church. We had a small kitchen, my husband Charles and I slept in the living room and the children all slept together in the bedroom. Shortly thereafter, we found housing in Altgeld Gardens where we had a living room, kitchen and three bedrooms.

Marcus was a happy and contented little baby that only cried when he was wet or hungry. That is why I was so surprised to find that he was born with a birth defect called Hemivertebrae, a condition where half of a vertebra in his spine didn't form. It occurs in less than one in 1000 births. In Marcus's case, it was found on the spinal cord in his neck. Two of his vertebrae weren't round like they were supposed to be. This deformity limited Marcus' range of motion in his neck. The doctors prescribed a brace for Marcus which he wore until he was about 4 years old. In all other developmental areas, Marcus was perfect.

Marcus is my only child that is left-handed. Statistics show that left-handed people are more successful in music and art and Marcus is definitely a gifted musician and artist. He taught himself to draw and sketch. He also taught himself to write with his right hand. He played the cornet in the band and orchestra in middle school and high school. The orchestra often accompanied many of the school plays and musicals. He was also a member of the high school marching band. Plus, Marcus played the cornet in a neighborhood band conducted by our friend and neighbor, Jerry Edison. This band went from door to door caroling during the Christmas season and other special occasions.

Scientist have long argued that left-handed people are more academically gifted because they use both sides of their brain. I am convinced that Marcus has a photographic memory. He never needed to study. He could read a document once and practically recite it back from memory. Marcus once told his sister that it was as if he could actually picture a document in his mind and then read it. I am convinced that Marcus is a genius. When he took the American College Test (ACT) he just missed making a perfect score (36) by a couple of points. I think a lot of his knowledge came from reading. He often read the Encyclopedia Britannica and National Geographic magazines. I am confident that these habits contributed to him being an honor roll student and getting inducted into the National Honor Society. One year, when he was in high school, he went on an anthropological dig with his science teacher. In fact, he appeared in a documentary on the Discovery Channel. He has always had a real thirst for knowledge.

In our family we had many "Game Nights." We enjoyed playing board games and one of the favorite games of the kids was Trivial Pursuit. The kids would often complain that they hardly got a turn because once Marcus took his turn, he was able to obtain all the "pieces of the pie" in one turn. Even his wild guesses were correct. His knowledge base was so broad that he was able to answer questions in all six categories easily; which are History, Science, Geography, Entertainment, Literature and Sports.

Marcus loves to cook. He is very competent in the kitchen and can make the best onion rings. Plus, he also bakes delicious cookies. He loved trying different things in the kitchen. One day he took the potato peeler and thinly sliced the whole potato and made potato chips. We thought they were as good as Lays Potato Chips.

Today it is very fashionable for young people to wear torn and distressed jeans or clothing. Marcus was the original designer of distressed clothing. I remember him taking perfectly good clothing and cutting or tearing them to create his own "look". He never allowed others to define who he is or how he should be. He is his own person and some might say that he is very eccentric.

Upon graduation from high school, Marcus enrolled in the University of Illinois in Champaign, Illinois. After completing several semesters there, he transferred to Columbia University in Chicago. Like the others, he was studious and strong academically.

It was here at Columbia University that he discovered his love for photography. While he was still learning photography, he offered to take family photos during a dinner at Aunt Katie's home. He brought all his photography equipment for his first family shooting. In an effort to soften the lighting in the room, Marcus took a napkin and covered his flash. He continued taking photos of all the family members present. When he developed the pictures several days later, he was surprised to find that his napkin solution to soften the lighting actually decreased the lighting in all the photos. In other words, the photos came out nearly black. While this photo session didn't produce the best "proofs" that day, Marcus has grown into an expert photographer. Marcus is the photographer who has taken some of my favorite photos of myself. Additionally, Marcus has taken senior and graduation photos of several family members that are truly cherished by their parents.

Marcus graduated with a Bachelor's Degree in Fine Arts. Just before his graduation ceremony, I told Marcus I'd buy him an outfit for his graduation. We went shopping and he bought a pair of shorts and a shirt. I don't care what kind of shirt Marcus had; he would cut the sleeves off. I asked him why he did this. He said, "I'm going to have a cap and gown on; what difference does it make?" Like I stated earlier, he has always been eccentric. On graduation day, he wore sandals, shorts, and the new shirt where he had cut off the sleeves, under his gown. This is typical Marcus, his own person.

After Marcus graduated, he decided to head west to live with his brother, Norris and his wife in Salina, California. He found a job that complimented his degree. Over the years, Marcus has done studio photography as well as in home photography. Additionally, he has been the photographer for an auto dealership highlighting the many vehicles in their fleet. After living in California and the state of Washington, Marcus and his family relocated to Houston then to Austin, Texas.

One of the most endearing things about Marcus that I cherish is his laughter. He has a heart-warming chuckle that stands out in the crowd. Hearing him laugh brings a smile to my face every time.

Marcus has two children, Mia and Ezra.

Above: *Top* - Mia, Lori and Marcus. My 70th Birthday party in 2011.

Bottom: *Left* – Ezra and Marcus. **Right** – Mia and Ezra.

Above: *Top* – Ezra, Lori and Mia 2020.
Bottom: *Left* - Mia 2009 Wedding. *Right* –Lori and Mia.

Sixteen

<u>Steven</u>

Above: Steven Anthony Major High School Senior Portrait 1982.

Steven is 16 months younger than Marcus. He is my fifth child. As a child, Steven was a very sensitive person and would cry at the drop of a hat. I'd tell him to go out and play, and he would go out and sit on the step. If someone walked by or a car started up, he'd get scared and cry. Steven is also very smart. When he was in the fourth or fifth grade, he had to write a paper. Years earlier I had purchased a set of Encyclopedia Britannica for my children to use to complete their homework. I worked very hard to pay for these encyclopedias, which were very pricey. Steven needed a picture to go with the story he was writing, so he cut the picture out of the encyclopedia. A couple of weeks later when I went to "open house" at Steven's school, there was my encyclopedia picture up there on the board. He got an "A" on his paper and was very proud of his work. We never did find out what kind of information was on the back of that picture.

Once when Steven was in about third grade, his teacher had her students write the recipes for their favorite meals. Steven made a cookbook out of his favorite recipes and gave it to me as a gift. I still have it and cherish his gift.

As a child, Steven was very curious. He would dissect snakes just to see what their insides looked like. Like most boys, he liked spiders and snakes and would chase his sister L'Tonya with them. His love for animals led him to putting his own clothes on our pet dogs. He was concerned about them being cold. Steven loved our pet dogs more than anyone in the family.

As the youngest boy, you would be surprised to learn that Steven was the child that picked on the other kids. He gave everyone nicknames and teased them often. As the baby of the family, I am sure L'Tonya received the brunt of his teasing.

While Steven was in high school, he started playing the tuba because the high school band did not have a tube player. The school loaned him a tuba, but it did not have a case, so I had to make him a carrying case. I pulled out my sewing machine and made a large denim bag, with a lining, for him to carry the instrument back and forth to school. Steven is a very gifted musician who also played the trombone.

We had a pretty good neighborhood organization, and they were always doing things for the children. One Christmas, Jerry Edison, who live across the street started a band. Jerry was actually enrolled in college at the time and was home for the holidays. Steven and Marcus both joined this neighborhood band. That year, Jerry as the conductor, and his band went door to door playing Christmas Carols to all the neighbors. This was a very loving and thoughtful gesture. Everyone enjoyed it.

Out of all my children who participated in Readers Theater and Drama, I believe that Steven won the most awards. His gift as an orator combined with his intelligence makes him a dynamic speaker. He performed in several plays and competed in theater competitions throughout high school.

In addition to Steven's artistic abilities, he also excelled academically. He is my other child that fell a few points short of making a perfect score on the ACT. His grades were exceptional and he was rewarded for his academic achievements. Steven was accepted into several Ivy League colleges to include Harvard, Princeton and Yale. Additionally, Steven was also accepted in several military academies to include the United States Military Academy West Point. After much deliberation over his many choices for a college education, Steven decided to attend the United States Coast Guard Academy in Groton, Connecticut. Steven was the first African American appointee to the U.S. Coast Guard Academy from the state of Illinois. During his senior year, Steven was selected and inducted into "Who's Who Among American High School Students". This organization recognized high school students who excelled in academics, extracurricular activities and service to others. Steven was also inducted into the National Honor Society at his high school. I was very proud of all that Steven had achieved in his young life.

Steven completed one year at the U. S. Coast Guard Academy and then decided to resign his appointment and eventually enlisted in the U.S. Army. The Army quickly recognized Steven's intelligence and sent him to the Defense

Language Institute (DLI) in Monterey California to learn and master the language of Korea. Steven was trained in the language of Hangul/Korean and served his country in the Military Intelligence branch. He spent much of his time translating information sent by the North Koreans.

After serving his country, Steven went to college to complete his degree. While attending the University of Alaska he became involved with the theatrical department. He appeared in a play named *"Conduct of Life"*, playing the part of Alejo. He also wrote an article for the Anchorage Times newspaper entitled "Get Your Motors Running." This was about a Rod and Custom Car Shows.

Utilizing his intelligence, Steven worked as a legal aid doing research for lawyers helping them prepare their cases. He also worked as a professor at the college level teaching political science and economics. Steven holds several Bachelor Degrees as well as a Master's Degree. My son Steven has the intelligence and capabilities to accomplish anything he sets his mind to do.

Steven is my only child who doesn't have any children . . . yet.

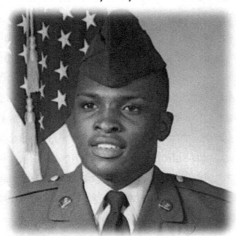 

Above: *Left* - Steven Anthony Major U. S. Army. ***Right*** - Steven 2020.

Above: Cadet Steven A. Major U. S. Coast Guard Academy 1982.

Above: Cadet Steven A. Major U. S. Coast Guard Academy 1982.

SEVENTEEN

L'TONYA

Above: L'Tonya Marie Major High School Senior Portrait 1985.

L'Tonya is my number six child. There are three years between Steven and L'Tonya. I always refer to her as "Major Six." She was a very sweet little baby who watched every move the other children made. L'Tonya was a fast learner who quickly learned from the other children. She learned what to do and what not to do. She was wise enough to not get in trouble. Everyone loved L'Tonya and protected her.

When I was pregnant with L'Tonya, Carol begged me to have a little girl. She even threatened to leave if I did not have a girl. She said she was tired of all these boys. That summer that I was due to have L'Tonya, I allowed Carol to spend the summer in Omaha with Little Mama. After L'Tonya was born, L'Tonya and I took the train to Omaha to pick up Carol and bring her home. I remember the pure joy and delight on Carol's little face when I presented her sister L'Tonya to her. Carol said, "Wow! She looks like a little Indian baby." L'Tonya had a cute little round face with straight black hair pasted to her head. I had to agree with Carol that L'Tonya did look like a little Indian doll baby. Although, Carol and L'Tonya were not twins, I dressed them the same all the time. They wore the same color clothing and the same hairstyles. I really enjoyed having two little girls that I could dress up.

As a little girl, L'Tonya enjoyed playing all sorts of games to include sneaking up on someone and scaring them by saying "Boo!" When L'Tonya was around four years old, I worked at Carver Elementary School. One day we had a teacher's planning day at school so the kids did not have class that day. As a way to thank the teachers for their hard work, our principal decided to have a potluck lunch for the teachers. I was responsible for making some cornbread muffins. I had melted the shortening (Crisco grease) and was getting ready to pour the hot grease in the muffin tin when L'Tonya sneaked up behind me, and said "Boo!" She actually scared me.

When I jumped the grease spilled out of the pan I was holding and landed on the top of L'Tonya's foot. This accident happened back when we were taught to put butter/margarine on burns. I took a stick of margarine and rubbed it on the burn. Thinking that I had rendered good first aid to my child, we continued to get ready for our day. We all got dressed and I took L'Tonya to her nursery school then I went on to work. At about 10:00 am, the nursery school called me and said, "Mrs. Major, you have to come to get L'Tonya. She has a blister on her foot. She's in a lot of pain and she's crying." I went to the nursery school and picked up L'Tonya and then took her to the County Hospital Emergency Room. They asked me how she was burned. I explained what happened, and the next thing I knew, the police and social workers were in the room. They ordered me to tell the story again. By this time, I was so upset, that I was crying. I kept telling them that I didn't burn her on purpose. That she had snuck up behind me and scared me while I was holding a pan with hot grease. When I jumped, the hot grease splashed on her foot. The policeman finally told the social worker, "That is probably what happened; she's not an abusive mother. You can tell by the appearance of her child."

I am positive that I was crying more than L'Tonya was crying. I honestly thought they were going to take my children from me. Thank God they could see that I was not an abusive mother and realized that this was a horrible accident. They kept L'Tonya in the hospital overnight because they wanted to do a skin graph on her the next day. Her wound was the size of a half-dollar piece. They replaced the burned skin with skin from her hip. I was so happy to take my child home that evening and I'm pretty sure L'Tonya never snuck up behind anyone else and yelled, "Boo!"

L'Tonya was a very passionate child and fiercely independent. Everything she did, she did with her whole heart. In Junior High School, she participated in the band and played the clarinet. She was a dedicated musician who could also sing. Once in high school, L'Tonya made the cheerleading squad and was an active member in Readers Theater and Drama. L'Tonya performed many weekends at high school competitions in Readers Theater. In Readers Theater, the student uses his/her voice to effectively communicate feelings, expressions, and emotions by enunciating and pronouncing words a certain way to communicate meaning. Also, the student doesn't use costumes, props or scenery to act; it's all in his or her words and how they convey them. From the beginning, L'Tonya was extremely effective in doing this. She was especially good at "Dramatic Interpretation". I believe that the skills that L'Tonya learned in Readers Theater are skills that she has applied throughout her life and continues to use to this very day. Even though L'Tonya is the youngest of my children, I think she is the one who matured the fastest and learned the quickest. She didn't make the mistakes my other children made. She has always made wise, mature decisions that were in alignment with what God's will was for her life.

One of the things that most impresses me about L'Tonya is her love for God. Even as a high school student, L'Tonya had a thirst for the word of God. She sought out Godly people and even chose her own church. As a teenager, she attended church on her own and made choices based on her own beliefs in accordance with what she believed God wanted her to do. It has always touched my heart to see her working to please God. It was no surprise to me when L'Tonya told me that she wanted to be a minister and servant of God.

After graduating from Alan B. Shepard High School in 1985, L'Tonya decided to attend college at Southern Illinois University (SIU) in Carbondale where Carol and Kelly once attended. During the spring semester of her freshman year at SIU, L'Tonya decided to enlist in the Army. At that same time, Carol was attending Northern Illinois University (NIU) working towards a second Bachelor's degree and decided to enlist in the Army too. Even though they were over 300 miles apart, they tried to enlist in the Army and attend basic training at the same time. Unfortunately, they weren't able to attend basic training at the same time. As it turned out, Carol finished basic training at Fort Jackson, South Carolina just as L'Tonya arrived at Fort Jackson to start basic training. As planned, they served their country together.

L'Tonya was an excellent soldier who took pride in being the best soldier she could be. Her job was in human resources, ensuring that soldiers received the pay and benefits they were entitled to. I think the soldiers who benefited the most from L'Tonya's vast knowledge were Carol and her soldiers. L'Tonya met and married her husband John while serving in the Army. She and John mentored and coached Carol throughout her Army career contributing greatly to Carol's successes in the Army. In many ways, L'Tonya became the big sister to Carol teaching her about the Army, marriage and parenting.

At one point in their military careers, both L'Tonya and Carol were stationed in Germany. I had the opportunity to visit and tour parts of Europe with both my girls while they served their country. Following their tour in Germany, both my daughters were stationed at Fort Hood, Texas. After serving her country for nearly eight years, L'Tonya decided to leave the service and focus on her family and education. She went back to school and graduated from Paul Quinn College with her Bachelor of Science Degree. This she did while raising three (3) children. Shortly after receiving her Bachelor's Degree, L'Tonya began a new career with the Veterans Administration in Waco, Texas. Utilizing her administrative skills and leadership skills from the U. S. Army, L'Tonya quickly was promoted through the ranks to a supervisory position. She is an incredible leader who ensures that veterans receive the benefits and services they are entitled to because of their service to our nation.

As I stated earlier, L'Tonya has always cultivated a relationship with God. She received her calling and was ordained a minister through the Potter's House. She utilizes the skills learned in Readers Theater to speak the Gospel to many to include family members. L'Tonya is a great minister and counselor. She spends much of her time counseling and ministering to friends, co-workers and our family. I often seek her counsel and value her opinions. Presently, L'Tonya is working on her Master's Degree and should complete it in the near future.

L'Tonya and John Allen have been married for well over three decades. The love that they have for each other is unmatched. They have shown our family what real love is and the beauty of true commitment. My prayer is that each of my children and their children would experience the same true love and respect that L'Tonya and John Allen have for one another. I thank God for bringing John Allen into L'Tonya's life. We all have been blessed by his love and generosity.

L'Tonya has three children, Ryan, Kaci and Alicia.

Above: John, Kaci, L'Tonya, Alicia and Ryan. **Bottom:** *Left* – SP4 L'Tonya Allen U. S. Army 1992. *Right* – Alicia and L'Tonya at Alicia's Sweet 16 Roaring 20s Party.

Above: John and L'Tonya My 70th Birthday Party in 2011.

Below: John, Kaci, Alicia, L'Tonya and Ryan.

Above: Alicia, Kaci, Ryan, John and L'Tonya. **Bottom:** *Left* – Alicia and Kaci 2009 Wedding. **Right** – Kaci, Ryan and Alicia.

Above: L'Tonya, Ryan, John, Alicia and Kaci.

Bottom: Ryan High School Graduate Portrait in 2009.

EIGHTEEN

BECOMING A HOMEOWNER

As a young mother during my marriage to Charles Major, we initially lived in a one-bedroom spacious apartment above a church. In 1965, Charles and I moved to Altgeld Gardens, a Chicago Housing Authority public housing project located on the far south side of Chicago, Illinois. This housing project sits on the border of Chicago and Riverdale, Illinois. It was built in 1943 for Black servicemen returning from World War II and their families. It still stands as a testament to good public housing design ideals, with low two-story buildings linked together in groupings and placed in a park-like setting. It has its own library, schools, churches, medical clinics and shopping. There were many great things about this housing project to include the close-knit community we had with our neighbors, church and schools. When Charles Major and I separated, I decided to look for new housing outside of the city limits.

I don't remember how I learned about the government program that sponsored the "235 Housing Program." In this program qualified low-income people with children, who worked, could purchase a home of their own. We only had to make a down payment of $235.00 towards the purchase of the home once fully qualified. My best friend Mrs. Janet Banks and I were on a house-hunting mission. We looked at home sites in nearby communities on the south side of Chicago like Robbins, Morgan Park and Roseland. Unfortunately, these home sites were mostly in areas where old homes had been demolished or had unkempt vacant lots all around them. Many of them were very close together, with no room to breathe, much like an apartment

Above: Altgeld Gardens Block 6 – Front Side. **Bottom:** Altgeld Gardens Block 6 – Back Side.

Above: *Top Left* – Christmas in Altgeld Gardens 1969. *Top Right* – My First Home. *Middle and Bottom Rows*: Images from My First Home.

building. A realtor told me about the houses that were being built in Robbins, Illinois. Robbins is a very small country suburb on the southwest side of Chicago. The vast majority of the people who live in Robbins are Black. At that time, Robbins had a population of about 13,000 people. I really liked the fact that these houses were not so close together. I choose a home that had a vacant lot on both sides.

It was a strange twist of fate that afforded me the opportunity to purchase my first home. After spending spring break in Omaha, Nebraska visiting my mother and siblings, my children and I were driving back home to Chicago. I exited the toll road at our exit on 127th Street in Alsip, Illinois. As I was driving down the street, a car made a sharp left turn in front of my car. As I slammed on the brakes to avoid hitting this car, I also quickly flung my arm across Carol and Norris who were riding in the front seat of my car to ensure they were not thrown into the windshield. Thinking I had avoided a collision, I was totally shocked and jolted forward when the car behind us, which was following too close, slammed into the back of our car. The lady that ran into the back of our car had just picked up her car from the auto body repair shop. The settlement from this accident was enough for the $235 down payment and my moving expenses.

Many people helped make our move possible. The maintenance man from L'Tonya's nursery school gave me enough paint to paint the inside of the house and a friend volunteered to paint it. All of this was done before we moved into our new home. This friend also drove the U-Haul on moving day. I can honestly say that I have been blessed with many wonderful people in my life that have helped me. I am truly thankful for their assistance.

In April 1971 my children and I moved into our new home and I became a homeowner. We lived on Lincoln Lane in Robbins, Illinois. I took much pride in my new home and enjoyed decorating and maintaining it. This was one of the greatest moments of my life. I was so grateful for what God had done in providing my children and I a new home.

There were so many things that I loved about our new home and community. We were out of the city and enjoyed country suburban life. We didn't have to lock our doors and my children could play outside without me having to worry about their safety. Our neighborhood was a new community where most of the neighbors had recently moved from the city of Chicago and had been approved for the 235 Housing Program too. There were about two dozen older homes scattered throughout our neighborhood that made up this community prior to the 235 Housing Program building our homes in this area. These homes were beautiful, well built, brick homes that housed some of the nicest people. Many of these homeowners became the foundational members of our neighborhood "Block Club". People like Mr. & Mrs. Wright, Mr. & Mrs. Chapman, Mr. & Mrs. Gaines, Mr. & Mrs. Ratcliff and Mr. & Mrs. Bunn mentored us new homeowners.

Our "Block Club" hosted many neighborhood events and activities for the families in our community. One of Norris' friends, Ronald "Ace" Chapman was actively engaged in developing the kids in our neighborhood. Even as a high school student at Harold L. Richards High School, Ace coached and mentored so many neighborhood kids. In fact, he coached Carol's softball team as well as other teams to include little league baseball. Ace was an incredible athlete who took pride in developing the kids in our neighborhood. As a champion of our children and sports, one year Ace convinced our Block Club Treasurer, Mr. Wright, to buy the sports equipment for our neighborhood teams. Ace was a very good speaker and advocate for our youth. Eventually Ace expanded his crusade for youth to include all the youth in the city of Robbins. After college, Ace became the Park Commissioner of Robbins and continued to mentor, coach and develop youth in the entire city of Robbins. As a direct result of Ace's gift in developing young athletes, many of his players had successful sports careers at the high school, college and professional level. There are many young athletes who were coached and developed by Ace Chapman to include a few athletes who eventually played professional sports.

Ace Chapman has been a dear friend of our family for over 50 years. To this day, Ace keeps our family informed about friends who still live in Robbins. His influence in the city of Robbins has been so great that many lovingly call him "The Mayor of Robbins".

After all my children graduated from high school and began their adult lives, I moved from my first home on Lincoln Lane in Robbins, Illinois, back into the city of Chicago in order to be near my aging father and his older sisters, Aunt Carrie and Aunt Katie. After retiring from the Chicago Board of Education, I moved to Waco, Texas to be near L'Tonya and help care for her children while she completed her college education.

Above: Ronald "Ace" Chapman 1979.

NINETEEN

FAMILY TRADITIONS

Above: *Top* – Kelly (5), Myself, Norris (6). *Bottom* – Carol (4), Steven (1) and Marcus (2). *Insert:* L'Tonya (4).

Tradition in my family is something I've never pondered. The dictionary states that tradition means "The passing down of elements of a culture from generation to generation, especially by oral communication."

In my family, when I was growing up, there were no family traditions that I can remember. As a mother, especially after we moved into our own home, we began several traditions. My children have always enjoyed "Family Game Night." We often spent many Saturday evenings just playing board games. We enjoyed Monopoly, Sorry, The Game of Life, Clue, and Trivial Pursuit. In addition, we played many card games like Spades, Uno, Go Fish, and War. Our family game nights gave us time together as a family and the opportunity to see a different side of each of my children. I was able to see who was competitive as well as which children were rivals. In addition, I also learned who would do anything to win to include cheating. Surprisingly, one of my daughters was the biggest cheater. To this very day, my children and I still have family game nights. Many Sundays after dinner we take advantage of this family tradition. And I am sure to keep my good eye on my daughter to ensure she is NOT cheating.

Another Family Tradition that I enjoyed with my children was Sunday afternoon drives. On Sunday mornings we worshipped together at my childhood friend's church. Reverend J. C. Wade, Jr. who was the pastor at Zion Missionary Baptist Church in East Chicago, Indiana. Every Sunday we would make the 45-minute drive to worship at his church. I'm not sure if our Sunday drives started because we were already on the road driving to and from church but we started enjoying afternoon drives. Sometimes we would just get in the car and I would drive. Other times I would ask the children which direction or town they would like to travel in. This tradition was inexpensive but so much fun. I would simply put $2 (two dollars) worth of gas in the tank of my car and drive. All of my children still enjoy road trips and my daughters to this very day still enjoy short afternoon trips. When they take these drives, they say that they are "Looking at Grass." I believe there is rest and enjoyment in such a simple pastime.

When I worked at Carver Primary School, the school was often given tickets to cultural events and activities in and around the Chicago land area. These tickets were given to the school in order to provide opportunities for low-income families to experience the many performing arts activities in Chicago. Our Principal, Dr. Alma Jones always offered these tickets to the parents of her students. When no other parents accepted the ticket, I would be gifted these tickets and would take my children to the performances. We received tickets to live theatric events, circuses, ice shows, museums, baseball games and the many cultural activities in the Chicago land area. All their lives, my children had the opportunity to enjoy theatrical performances at the highest level. This tradition continues to this day, especially with my daughters. We attend plays and shows of many genres to include musicals, circuses, mystery theaters, high school plays and so many other events. We have even been to Broadway plays in New York and Las Vegas shows to include Cirque Du Soleil's infamous "O", "The Lion King", and "The Colored Purple". If there is a show in town that interests us, we are going to see it.

When my children were little and I lived in Chicago, I started the holiday tradition of a family dinner. Most Thanksgiving dinners were at my new home in Robbins. I would take off Monday thru Wednesday of Thanksgiving week. We spent the week cleaning the house, cooking and baking. On Thanksgiving morning, the round-ups began. Because the "seniors" (Daddy, Aunt Carrie, Aunt Katie and Uncle White) did not drive, I had to play taxi and pick them all up. My father lived on the north side of Chicago so I picked him up first. It was a one-hour drive, one way to his house. Aunt Carrie was the second pick up on the south side, and Aunt Katie and Uncle White were the third stop. After gathering everyone, we enjoyed a wonderful dinner and fellowship with each other.

The children were asked about their school activities, and when they finished explaining everything, Aunt Carrie would always say, "Ya'll too smart for me." She also called them "Mister/Miss Brain". I think her interest in their activities made them study harder because they always wanted to impress Aunt

Carrie. I firmly believe that this tradition was a key part of my children's success in school and helped mold their futures. We kept this tradition every year until the children all left home.

After moving to Texas, we revived the family tradition with an adjustment because the children were all married and had their own families. We now celebrate Thanksgiving the week before Thanksgiving, allowing daughters-in-law and sons-in-law to be with their own families on Thanksgiving. We also rotate who will host the dinner - North Texas, Central Texas, or South Texas. Almost all of my children now live in Texas.

Instead of one person preparing the entire Thanksgiving Day meal, we split the responsibility. Everyone brings a dish. Evada is Norris' wife and has a standing invitation to make the "potato salad." My family believes that she makes the best potato salad EVER! Which has resulted in the fact that we now have potato salad thieves in the family, so she has to make 15-20 pounds of potato salad so that anyone who wishes can take some home. Thereby eliminating the need for people to hide and stash potato salad once it arrives on site.

I am the family baker. I usually bake a "Five Flavor Pound Cake" and Sweet Potato Pies. Normally I will also have to bake a few small pound cakes to be taken home for later. The recipe for these treats can be found in the back of this book along with an entire Thanksgivings Day meal. My youngest daughter L'Tonya has an excellent start of taking over my baking skills, so look out, family.

When Carol and L'Tonya were stationed in Germany for three years, they wanted to continue this family tradition so they asked me to write down my Thanksgiving Day recipes to include illustrations and send them to them in Germany. So, I did exactly that. To this day, they use my recipes when they prepare any of these food items for Thanksgivings Day or any other day. I have included these recipes in this book so that you can enjoy these flavorful dishes and desserts.

When we gather together on Thanksgiving Day, we enjoy each other as a family and as individuals. We lift each other up and encourage one another. We exchange ideas (tips) on parenting, finances, and everyday survival. In addition, we solve world issues. Through all of this, we have learned to value and celebrate one another to include our differences.

Above: *Left* – Cynthia, Carol, Marcus, Carmela, Norris, L'Tonya, Carlett, Steven and Kelly. *Right* – Daddy, Carrie Mae, James Cunningham, Me and Norris. *Bottom* – Cousins in Memphis 1975.

TWENTY

LOCKHART ACADEMY - REORGANIZATION

When I moved to Chicago in 1960, I became a student and resident at "Lockhart Academy." The instructors at Lockhart Academy, Aunt Carrie and Aunt Katie, were a balm for my weary soul. The life lessons I learned under Aunt Carrie and Aunt Katie were invaluable. They gave me a "leg up" in life and prepared me to be a good citizen, responsible parent, and loving friend. My aunts who were the instructors at the "Lockhart Academy" were my angels. They lifted me when I felt like I was drowning and taught me that I still could be somebody in spite of my past or the choices I had made.

Aunt Carrie also helped me to heal and forge relationships that would be lasting and beneficial. Next, she taught me how to be a woman and responsible mother. She helped me to understand the importance of being a good provider for my children and to love myself.

Lockhart Academy was not an accredited school, just a safe and nonjudgmental home that gave me love and guidance. Ultimately, I finished high school, got married, and found gainful employment, where I worked for the next 30 years. Finally, I purchased a home and earned an Associate Degree.

I suppose I expected the Lockhart Academy to close its doors when both founders passed away; I assumed the school was gone too. But, as I look back over our family members' lives, I can see fragments of the academy appearing today as strong as ever.

The revived "Lockhart Academy" is comprised of the next generation of family leaders and mentors. These new leaders are God-believing, Spirit-filled loving family members that includes the Kings, the Strongs, and the Allens, who are now helping the next generation of young people develop into capable, responsible adults. They are helping them to look at the challenges they face and providing them with resources to work them out. They are in tune with this generation. Norris and Kelly, aka "Lockhart Academy - Kings Incorporated" were the first new branches that opened decades ago. As adults, they quickly took their younger siblings under their wings and began coaching and mentoring them when they faced life's challenges. In many instances, they provided financial support, a place to live and sound coaching in order to help assist their younger siblings with standing on their own two feet. They have been true big brothers to their younger siblings on many occasions.

The "Lockhart Academy" now has a new branch known as "Allen and Strong Incorporated." This branch has brought back memories of my life and some of the lessons that I learned. Carol and L'Tonya have replaced Aunt Carrie and Aunt Katie. They are strong branches stemming from the Lockhart Academy. When family members need guidance and assistance, they have teamed together to help. Their presence and participation are a strong testimony and visible contribution of the Lockhart Academy's love. The two of them have helped many family members dealing with different life challenges.

The generosity that my children extend to each other and other family members has been impressive. It touches my heart to see other family members receiving the love and support from the new Lockhart Academy. It makes me proud to see the legacy of Aunt Carrie and Aunt Katie passing from generation to generation. I commend all those who strive to keep the Lockhart Academy alive and relevant. To them I say: "Keep up the good work, save our family!"

Above: "Lockhart Academy Reorganized" – Carol Strong and L'Tonya Allen.

TWENTY-ONE

WORK AND CAREER

When my children were little and attended Carver Primary School, I would volunteer at their school. My volunteer work led to the school offering me a permanent position. I was hired to be a School Community Representative (SCR). I held this position for 30 years and retired from the Chicago Board of Education in 1997.

As a SCR, I was a liaison between the school and the community. I worked with the parents to help foster a better relationship between them and the school. I reported directly to the principal as a SCR. I was responsible for meeting with community organizations and individuals to explain and respond to inquiries concerning various school programs and activities. I consulted with the educational staff to obtain information concerning teachers' interest and concerns and communicated this information to the community members. It was also my responsibility to know the community organizations and social service agencies and their programs and policies. I attended community meetings, workshops and activities related to educational matters and meet with community leaders and business representatives that solicited the support of the school and our programs. Additionally, I communicated directly with parents to encourage their children's regular attendance at school and parent participation in school activities.

Moreover, I also helped those parents who needed to finish high school, get their diplomas. Some even completed college. I also taught them how to conduct a business meeting, according to "Robert's Rule of Order". Often, I helped them write speeches to present at the Chicago Board of Education public hearings where they could address their concerns for our school. My job as a SCR was perfect for me. I truly enjoyed being an active part of my children's school and intimately involved in my community. Through my job, I established many lasting relationships and feel that I was an important part of my children's educational experience.

While I had many memorable experiences, as a SCR at Carver Primary Elementary School, one of the best experiences I had was the pleasure of meeting and working with a Community Activist. President Obama was one of the young men my principal, Dr. Alma Jones, mentored. He often visited our school and community. In the movie, "Southside with You", President Obama takes First Lady Michelle Obama on their first date, which included attending a community meeting in Altgeld Gardens. When Senator Obama was running for president in 2008, he hosted a Town Hall Meeting at the American Legion Post here in Houston, Texas. After the meeting which Carol and her husband Garrick attended, she had the opportunity to meet and speak with then Senator Obama. I had instructed Carol to tell Senator Obama that Mrs. Major from Carver Primary said hello. When Carol told Senator Obama that I said hello, he responded, "Mrs. Major is your mother?" I was so touched that he remembered me.

Shortly after retiring from Carver Primary as a SCR, I moved to Texas. Once here in Texas, I took a part-time job working at J.C. Penny in Waco. One of the main reasons I moved to Texas was to help care for L'Tonya's children as she completed her Bachelor's Degree. When Carol transferred to Prairie View A&M University just north of Houston to be the Professor of Military Science in 2004, I was close enough to help with caring for her daughter, Sydni, when her husband Garrick was deployed to Iraq.

I have been blessed with retirement benefits from the Chicago Board of Education as well as occasional gifts from my children. Together these blessings allow me to truly enjoy retirement.

Above: *Left* – Me with Co-Worker at JCPenney. *Right* – Aid to Senator Obama, Carol, then Senator Obama, Michelle, Garrick, Mark and Soloria at a Town Hall Meeting in Houston, Texas at the American Legion in February 2008.

Above: Carver Primary Staff 1979.

TWENTY-TWO

LOSS OF A FRIEND

One of my dearest friends was Mrs. Janet Banks. I met Janet Banks when I volunteered with the Parent Teachers Association (PTA) at Carver Primary School. We both lived in the same housing project in Chicago, Altgeld Gardens. She was the first School Community Representative (SCR) hired at the Carver Primary School. A few months after they hired Janet, I too was interviewed for a SCR position. When they offered me the position, I gladly accepted and spent the next 30 years of my life as a SCR.

Janet and I worked well together and became great friends. We had children that were the same age and they became great friends as well. We made a great team. Like many schools today, the elementary school (Carver Primary), the middle school (Carver Junior High School) and high school (Carver High School) were all located together in a cluster. There was a total of five SCRs amongst all the schools in our cluster. The five SCRs became very close because of our work and we were active members of our community.

As a result of Janet and I working together, our friendship grew. As the years passed, my friendship with Janet grew closer and closer. We shared life together to include hardships and triumphs. One summer the school did not need SCRs and we were forced to apply for unemployment. Our friendship was so strong that we always ensured that neither of our families did without. We took care of one another.

When Janet was diagnosed with breast cancer, we were devastated. She lived for another year and a half. One of the most difficult things to do is to watch a loved one die. It was heart wrenching to watch the disease of breast cancer and the effects of chemotherapy destroy my friend's body. She was a strong fighter to the end. The same weekend that Janet passed, my neighbor, Betty Edison, who lived across the street, also passed away from breast cancer. This was one of the saddest times in my life.

Janet not only was my co-worker, but she was also my confidant, and my best friend. We did so much together to including traveling together and sharing recipes. I miss Janet even to this day because we could talk about anything and tell each other everything. We discussed world issues and talked about growing old and what it would be like being grandparents. What I miss most about her was having a confidant that I could tell about my children. In truth, we were more like sisters.

After Janet's passing, I did not develop another close friendship like that until I moved to Texas. I started attending church services at Pleasant Olive Missionary Baptist Church in Waco, Texas. While serving in mission together I met a wonderful lady named Ms. Rosetta Thompson. We quickly became friends because we had so much in common. She was a very caring individual who enjoyed serving on the mission team. Often, we would serve together at different church events. Our friendship lasted about three years before Rosetta became critically ill and eventually died. Losing my friend Rosetta was a difficult loss as well. It seems the older you get, the more you experience loss. While I am grateful for the longevity of my life, I definitely miss the friends and love ones that have passed before me.

Above: Carver Primary Staff – 1972. **Center:** My dear friend, Mrs. Janet Banks, is highlighted in the center of photo. I am one row behind Janet and to her right.

TWENTY-THREE

FAITH AND SPIRITUALITY

When my brother, sister and I lived to Memphis, Tennessee with my paternal grandparents, I remember attending church with Maw Maw and Paw Paw. My grandfather, Walter King (Paw Paw) was a minister and we attended church at Greater White Stone Missionary Baptist Church, which was around the corner from our house.

Once we moved to Omaha, Nebraska, my siblings and I began attending church with our mother. We started worshiping at Salem Missionary Baptist Church because our next-door neighbors had invited us to their church. Still to this day, my family members who live in Omaha continue to worship at Salem Missionary Baptist Church. Reverend J. C. Wade, Senior was the pastor when we joined the church in 1948.

Even though my mother didn't speak about her faith often, she was an active member in the church. My mother and Little Mama attended church regularly and ensured that we also attend church and knew the teachings of Jesus Christ. Mama was on the Usher Board, Mission Board and was a "Nurse's Aid". Many times, we also attended mid-week services on Wednesday nights. My mother was even elected to serve as the President of the Usher Board. I along with my siblings sang in the choir and served on the Junior Usher Board. I also participated in most Junior Church Activities and played in the church orchestra.

One day after witnessing my mother place money in the offering, I asked her why she only placed a dollar ($1) in the offering plate. She replied, "Because

I only need a dollar worth of faith." As a child I did not understand what she meant by this; I was baffled for years by her response.

Faith to me is something that grows with you as you experience life and walk with the Lord. The more you study His word and see God moving in your own life, the more you develop faith. It was very important to me to give my children a foundation of Jesus Christ.

Jesus told his disciples in Matthew 7:20 that if they only had faith the size of a mustard seed, they could simply speak to a mountain and tell it to move and it would move. He said that nothing would be impossible for them if they only had faith the size of a mustard seed.

Over the years my faith has grown. As a young adult, I struggled to see God in my life, especially when I was in the middle of one of life's storms. But now when I look back over my life, I can see God actively moving in my life and my children's life. I can now see how God has protected us and how He goes before us. I can see the good health and long life He has blessed me with. I can see how He made a way out of no way so many times. I can see how He blesses me financially and how He places just the right person in my path. I can see how He opens doors for me. I can see how He blesses me even when I don't deserve His blessings. Even when I don't see Him working, I know that He is working behind the scenes of my life. This is faith.

In the King James Bible, Hebrews 11:1 says "Now faith is the substance of things hoped for, the evidence of things not seen." What this means to me is that faith is having the assurance about something that you will see later. Believing in the evidence of what we have not seen requires faith. When I trust that God will do something, this is exercising my faith. At times when I am hoping that God will do something, I must also believe that which I have not yet seen. This is faith and the foundation of my spirituality. Faith is not fear. Faith is assurance. Faith is a knowing that God will step in.

Writing this book has been an act of faith and a true spiritual journey. Throughout my life's journey, my faith has been tested many times. God has been faithful and has sustained me even during the most difficult days. I have been so blessed. When I look back on my life, I can honestly say that God has been faithful throughout my life's journey. I am so grateful that God has always loved me and protected me on my journey.

TWENTY-FOUR

EPILOGUE

To my children, grandchildren, great grandchildren and future generations,

I pray that when you have finished reading this book you will understand me better, learn from my mistakes and build on the great legacies of our family. Let the world know that you come from good stock, you are from Rosemary's branch and that we are a force to be reckoned with.

When my children were growing up and were forced to face life's challenges, I often told them, "That's your little red wagon. You can pull it full or empty. But Baby, you are going pull it." What I meant by this statement was that regardless of what challenges you face in your life; they are your challenges and you must decide how you will deal with those challenges. We must individually learn how to navigate life's roads and journeys.

As I have grown closer to Jesus Christ, I realize that my life has been the plan that God had for me. I now know that God allowed me to go through many challenges on this journey so that He could grow me and draw me closer to Him. I have learned to trust and lean on God.

Writing this book and recalling my life over the years has caused me to reflect on the many different experiences I have had. I am so appreciative and thankful for what God has brought me to and through.

When I graduated from Carver High School in 1967, I was selected to be our "Class Representative" and spoke at our graduation on behalf of all the graduates. In my speech I said, "Progress comes from looking forward, not backward. . . . We must continue to look forward to new things ahead." I challenge each of you to always look forward in life. Don't let your past mistakes define you. Keep moving forward, achieving one goal after another building your own legacy. It is my prayer that each generation that follows me becomes better than the previous generation.

I love you all!
Mama, Grandmeir, Rosemary

TWENTY-FIVE

SPECIAL THANKS

I am truly grateful to all those who helped make this book become a reality. I am especially grateful to my writing Coach Jackie Devine and my daughter Carol. Without their help, encouragement and assistance this book would have never come to be. Thank you both for everything you did to make this book a reality. I truly appreciate you both!

Twenty-Six

ROSEMARY'S RECIPES

Over the years, we have spent many hours gathered around the table. When we come together around the family table, we are making decisions, creating dreams, sharing good times and bad. During the holidays, we have certain dishes, which are a part of our celebrations. Here are a few that you grew up with and will often find at our family gatherings.

TURKEY AND CORNBREAD DRESSING

This recipe works best for a 10-12 pound turkey (thawed).

STEP 1:

CORNBREAD

1 ¾ cups of cornmeal

¼ cup flour

2 teaspoons baking powder

2 eggs

1 cup milk

¼ cup cooking oil

Mix cornmeal, flour, and baking powder together. Add eggs and milk then beat until well blended. Next heat the cooking oil in the pan that you are going to bake the cornbread in. Pour the hot oil into the mixture and stir well and then pour the mixture into pan and bake at 350 degrees until the cornbread is golden brown.

STEP 2:

DRESSING

1 ½ cups chopped celery

1 cup chopped onions

1 cup chopped green peppers

½ teaspoon garlic powder or one clove of garlic

1 tablespoon sage (very important).

2 cans of broth

8 slices of toast

1 stick of butter

In a skillet or microwave, melt ½ stick of butter, sauté onions, green peppers, and celery. Cook until all are transparent.

STEP 3:

BROTH

2 cups of water

½ stick of butter

2 tablespoons of chicken bullion powder

Break cornbread up into small pieces. Cut toast into pieces. Add cooked celery, onions, and green peppers. Mix in garlic (or powder). Or combine with the broth. You may have to add more sage, but first, taste it. Your mixture may be kind of soupy. That's okay. In the skillet or heat some oil. Pour in dressing mixture. Cook until thick (dry like).

Notice, I don't have salt anywhere. The bullion is salty, so be careful. Also, you may wish t use Mrs. Dash seasoning.

STEP 4:

TURKEY TIME

Wash the turkey. Clean out the cavity removing all fat and that red stuff in the back. Sprinkle the inside with seasoning then fill with dressing. Oh yes, the turkey should have a piece of skin that is hanging off up by the wings, do not cut that off and do not cut off the butt (tail)

Also, fill the cavity where the skin is extra-long with stuffing too. Sprinkle salt, paprika on the outside of the turkey. Rub with cooking oil. Fold the wings back. Pull the extra skin back and under the turkey. The wings should hold the excess skin in place. On the other end, put the drum sticks in the butt cavity. It should look like this:

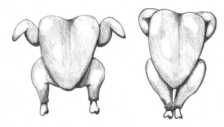

Back at 325 degrees for 2 ½ hours. Turkey should be starting to brown after 2 hours of baking.

Baste every half hour using drippings from the turkey.

If you have a roaster, cook covered. If not, cover with aluminum foil.

The liver, neck and gizzards may be boiled together. You may use the broth from this to make the broth and gravy. If you do this, put seasoning in it.

You may use the drippings from the turkey for the gravy.

STEP 5:

GRAVY

Pour 2 tablespoons of oil into a skillet.

Stir in 2 tablespoons of flour in a skillet, stir until golden brown. Add 1 ½ to 2 cups of broth.

Stir constantly until smooth. Cook until desired thickness.

Ham

If you are using a canned ham, get a good Polish one.

Glaze

½ cup brown sugar

½ cup honey

Mix honey and sugar

If using a canned ham, heat about 45 minutes, then add glaze.

If using a ham with a bone in it, cook 1 to 1 ½ hours, pour off drippings, then add a glaze, cook 15-20 minutes longer.

SWEET POTATO PIE

4 or 5 medium potatoes

Boil unpeeled until done. Run cold water on potatoes while you are peeling them. Cut potatoes crosswise. See illustration below. This is very important. Otherwise, you will have pies like Grandmother's. ☺

1 stick butter

1 to 1 ½ cups sugar

1 ½ teaspoons nutmeg

1 ½ teaspoons vanilla

½ teaspoon cinnamon

4 eggs

1 cup evaporated milk

2 frozen pie crust shells

After cutting the potatoes crosswise (the potatoes should still be warm), put butter into the bowl. Mash potatoes, add sugar, nutmeg, vanilla, and milk.

Beat eggs thoroughly, add to mixture and pour into pie shells. While mixing, taste for sweetness before adding the last ½ cup of sugar.

Bake at 350 degrees for one hour until crust or brown.

Sour Cream Pound Cake

2 ¾ cups sugar

1 cup butter

6 eggs

3 cups cake flour

½ teaspoon salt

¼ teaspoon baking soda

1 cup sour cream

½ teaspoon lemon extract

½ teaspoon vanilla extract

½ teaspoon orange extract

Cream together sugar and butter until light and fluffy. Add eggs one at a time beating well after each addition. Sift together flour, salt and baking soda; add to creamed mixture, alternating with sour cream, beat after each addition. Add extracts and beat well. Pour batter into greased and floured 10" tube (bundt) pan. Bake at 350 degrees for 1 ½ hours. Cool 15 minutes then remove from pan. When completely cool, frost or sprinkle with confection sugar if desired.

FIVE FLAVOR CAKE

3 cups sugar

2 sticks of butter or margarine

½ cup of vegetable shortening

5 eggs well beaten

3 cups cake flour

½ teaspoon baking powder

1 cup milk

1 teaspoon coconut flavor

1 teaspoon lemon flavor

1 teaspoon vanilla flavor

1 teaspoon rum flavor

1 teaspoon butter flavor

Cream together butter, shortening and sugar until light and fluffy. Add eggs which have been beaten until lemon colored. Combine flour and baking powder then add creamed mixture alternating with the addition of the milk. Beat well. Pour batter into greased and floured 10" tube (bundt) pan. Bake at 325 degrees for 1 ½ hours. Cool 15 minutes then remove from pan. When completely cool add glaze if desired.

FIVE FLAVOR CAKE – GLAZE

1 cup sugar

½ cup water

1 teaspoon coconut flavor

1 teaspoon lemon flavor

1 teaspoon vanilla flavor

1 teaspoon rum flavor

1 teaspoon butter flavor

1 teaspoon almond flavor

Combine ingredients in a heavy sauce pan. Stir well until sugar is melted. Bring to a boil. Pour half of the glaze over the cake while cake is still in the bundt pan and pour the other half of the glaze over the cake after you have removed it from the bundt pan. Enjoy.

LEMON-LIME SODA CAKE

3 cups sugar

1 ½ cups butter

5 eggs

3 cups cake flour

1 tablespoon lemon flavor

¾ cup of lemon-lime soda

3 teaspoons of lemon juice

LEMON-LIME SODA CAKE - ICING

3 cups of powdered sugar

1 tablespoon lemon flavor

1 teaspoon of vanilla flavor

½ cup of milk

Cream together sugar and butter until light and fluffy. Add eggs one at a time beating well after each addition. Fold in flour, lemon-lime soda and lemon juice. Pour batter into greased and floured 10" tube (bundt) pan. Bake at 325 degrees for 1 hour and 15 minutes. While cake is cooking, prepare icing. Icing: Mix all ingredients together and stir well.

Once cake is finished cooking, remove cake from oven. While cake is still warm and still in the bundt pan, punch holes in the cake and drizzle icing (about ¾ cup) over the warm cake. Next remove the warm cake from the bundt pan. Allow cake to cool for 15 minutes. Drizzle the remainder of the icing over the cake after it cools.

TWENTY-SEVEN

FINAL THOUGHTS OF WRITING COACH

Helping Rosemary tell her story has offered me an unforgettable adventure, with all the components of an award-winning novel: evocative, entertaining, historically accurate, and with an equal element of joy and sadness.

Rosemary gives us a unique and vividly dramatic first-hand glimpse into our rapidly diminishing mid-twentieth-century Black American history with extraordinary skill.

It took us almost two years to travel together down memory lane because each time she unpacked a piece of her historical family luggage, I became immersed in the depth of her experience and the extent of her knowledge and prodded her for more.

Now that it is complete, Rosemary's Journey proves what everyone who knows her can already attest: She is a survivor! They are right. However, I'm convinced she is who she is because of the females in her life that helped strengthen her to the core. They were all strong-willed, determined, intelligent, courageous, stubborn, humorous, and generous. Aunt Carrie and Aunt Katie were her angels. Rosemary has given you a peek into the soul of each of these ladies.

Still, of all the ladies that stoked Rosemary's fire, however, Little Mama lit my flame. Living in the deep south during the Roaring '20s, that beautiful, talented entrepreneur figured a way to cash in on the system. Yes, she reaped the rewards, but she also paid the penalty. After she paid her dues, as a member of the unrecognized migration out of the south, she high-tailed it out of Jim Crow territory, testing the waters in Kansas City and ending up in Omaha, Nebraska.

There she invested in a sizable home, large enough to accommodate her daughter, four grandchildren, and friends when they needed a place to live. In her tiny kingdom, she set the standard for how all others under her roof would live life. She was a talented seamstress, gifted designer, and brilliant orator. When she spoke, others listened. We may be two ships that passed in the night, via the mighty river Rosemary, but her memory has been forever forged in my heart.

Thank you, my dear Rosemary, for allowing me to hold your hand along life's way and support you in creating a legacy for your children that will live through eternity.

Writing Coach,

Jackie Devine

.